Challenge to Crisis

Challenge
to
Crisis

by
Melford Pearson

1969
Noblesville Indiana

Order this book online at www.trafford.com
or email orders@trafford.com

Most Trafford titles are also available at major online book retailers.

Printed in the United States of America.

ISBN: 978-1-4669-7083-0 (sc)
ISBN: 978-1-4669-7082-3 (e)

Trafford rev. 02/08/2013

 www.trafford.com

North America & international
toll-free: 1 888 232 4444 (USA & Canada)
phone: 250 383 6864 ♦ fax: 812 355 4082

CONTENTS

PREFACE

THIS small volume is written for those people in America who are willing to confront with realism and courage the serious problems facing this nation and the world. Its contents are not for the timid or the fanatical. Its pleadings leave no room for dogma, prejudice or maudlin sentimentality. It appeals only to those who possess both the desire and the will to solve our problems.

This book is motivated by the simple and urgent desire to consider candidly and honestly where and how we as a people have gone astray in working out our well-being and in shaping our destiny. More importantly, it is an attempt to apply rational concepts of human relationships in solving our problems so that each and every life takes on meaning and all the social institutions serve man instead of controlling him.

The writer of this volume has no professional standing in the subject matter covered. Nor is he a person with literary distinction. Perhaps, however, this is a fortuitous circumstance. There are no degrees to uphold; there are no institutions to be protected; there are no status symbols to be maintained. You as the reader are asked to accept what is offered only if it rings true with your own reasoning and conscience. The judgment must rest with you. Only bear in mind that it is the people themselves who are both benefactors and beneficiaries in working out their existence and their future. IN the final analysis, the supreme power rest with the people irrespective of their failure to exercise their inherent omnipotence.

Read the ensuing pages with an open mind and heart. Perchance together we can envision the prosperous, safe, dynamic America that awaits only our collective will to act forthrightly!

INTRODUCTION

I N WRITING this book the author is very mindful of the fact that he is dealing with subject matters which have been dealt with by learned men up in the centuries. He is also familiar with many writers of this Twentieth Century who have grappled with the problems of human relationship. Further, he has personal acquaintance with men of this current decade who are sincerely endeavoring to promote a better understanding of man's role in society.

This book is not written as a critique of all such writings. Nor is it written in a vein of criticism. It is an attempt by one person to extract the best from all that he has read, project his own thoughts, and apply such composite yardstick to considering mankind's problems of the present. In such an approach this writer can only express gratitude for the insights he has gleaned from the writing of many contributors to a more comprehensive understanding of man and his social structures.

There will be no attempt to make this a "documentary" book, although the writer has exercised great care to be as accurate as possible in presenting facts and figures. Documentation in the way of innumerable footnotes only tends to confuse and distract the reader. A selected bibliography is presented at the end of the book with the plea that each reader acquaints himself with a more thorough background of the thinking and persuasions related to in this writing.

It is the position of this writer that it is ideas that are of prime importance and not the men who expressed them. It is also here contended that it is only as we are able to translate ideas, or concepts, into just and workable human relationship within literal social structures that the worth of such ideas is determined. Otherwise they fall simply in the arena of philosophical abstractions without practical application.

Since man first set foot on this planet, the basic challenge to mankind has always been the same. Shorn of all its nonessentials, it reduces to this fundamental question: **How securely does man survive and how well does he survive?** Translated into a broader context, we are concerning ourselves with the efficiency with which mankind's needs are met and with the satisfaction with which people's urges are fulfilled.

Relating survival to practical reality, we confront and consider every aspect of man's day-to-day existence. Here we judge man's survival potential on his ability to provide food for himself and his family, on his ability to be secure in a home and furnish adequate clothing, on his ability to avail himself and his family of needed medical care when sick or injured, on his ability to get an adequate education, and on being able to enjoy the added benefits of recreation and travel.

Expanding survival to its fullest encompassment, we are considering man's opportunity for a lifetime pursuit of knowledge that he might enjoy increased spiritual harmony in appreciating his relationship to his fellowmen and the whole of creation.

It should not be difficult to realize that optimum survival would mean the fullest utilization of a nation's resources, of its science and technology, and of its productive machinery, all geared to fulfilling the foregoing requirements of each and every citizen. In such environment man's well-being and survival would be at its highest possible level. Of course, this must mean the absence of war which is contra-survival and destructive of life itself.

This writer knows that only the abysmally ignorant, those who callously profit by want and misery, and fools, are oblivious to the dangerous environment in which mankind is engulfed. Progressive breakdown confronts us whichever way we turn. Millions are denied work, tens of millions are living in want, the rate of crime exceeds the growth of population, more homes, small businesses and farms are being foreclosed on than at any time in the history of the nation, and a whole people staggers under an ever-spiraling load of taxation and indebtedness. And if such threats to man's survival aren't enough, the major powers in the world are insanely bent on increasing their nuclear arsenals until the globe itself is a lethal powder-keg whose hellish potential, deliberately or accidentally fused, could wipe out all existing life.

Crisis impends with a vengeance!

This book is not concerned with covering the technical advancements of mankind from the time of the caveman to that of modern man. There are many excellent books that cover in details the fashioning of the first crude clubs to ward off the wild beasts, the discovery of the wheel and axle, and the developments in both science and technology that have led to jet airliners and automated industries. It will, however, fully consider in its proper place the current explosive age of cybernation that we have entered and the capability that exits to provide a life of abundance for all citizens, heretofore not dreamed of in our wildest imaginings.

This book is primarily concerned with considering man as a human being and analyzing the economic and political systems he lives under, including the institutions which have been set up by him and now govern his movements, his conduct and to a large extent, his thought. Only in so doing will the reforms become apparent that should be made so that the sovereign people can shape their own lives and make the freedom and enhancement of human beings paramount in all relationship.

Man has become the victim of the very institutions and systems that he thought had been set up to serve and benefit him.

The writer of this book is fully aware that to attack the built-in evils of our capitalistic economic system, to challenge the right of the whole privately owned banking structure to issue a nation's credit, to charge that the monopolistic industrial cartels are interested only in exorbitant profits for the few, to indict the major political parties as the "front men" for the foregoing power structures, and to show no toleration for churchianity that does very little to practice the precepts it professes, is to invite every form of ridicule or malignant of character or general harassment the threatened powerblocs can devise. Such is the penalty for attacking the "sacred" institutions by which mankind has been bondaged and made serfs on their own acres.

However, any price is worth paying if one's contribution serves in some small measure to restore sanity to conducting the affairs of one's nation, and to making a safe and just society.

We are a nation predominantly of young people. Tens of millions of our boys and girls are approaching adulthood unaware of the usurers waiting to saddle them with debt, unaware that they are being educated for employment that won't exist, and unaware that the whole economy is held intact by a perpetual preparedness for, or embroilment in, needless wars. What meaningful opportunity exists for these millions of youngsters to enter our adult society unless drastic alterations are made in our whole economic arrangement? Or unless an abrupt halt is made to our nation's role in senseless and brutal slaughter involving the sacrifice of our best manhood.

Throughout the land some 30 million of the nation's citizens live in conditions of dire poverty in this, the richest country in the world. Current hearings and investigations, this spring of 1969, by the Senate Committee on Nutrition and Human Needs leave no room for questioning the fact that not only does widespread poverty stalk the land but millions actually suffer the pangs of hunger as a continuing affliction. This Committee estimates that 8 million Americans now live in families whose total income, including welfare payments, is less than half the Federally established "poverty level" and less than the amount which their own government estimates they need to meet their food needs alone. These are the victims of acute malnutrition.

Amidst warehouses bulging with foodstuffs and under the eyes of farmers paid not to produce, these forgotten Americans live in every part of our nation. They live, or more accurately exist, in the ghettos of our cities, on Indiana reservations, in migrant labor camps, or are hopelessly marooned in the Appalachias of the country. A callous nation has offered no real help in rescuing these hapless fellow humans from distresses for which they are not responsible, and has opened for them no opportunity to find a minimal degree of joy and dignity in life.

Amongst these pauperized tens of millions are some four millions of our citizens who have no weekly paychecks, despite the fact that nearly four million men are in the armed services and a good 10% of the entire labor force is engaged in defense industries. These are the unemployed, the able-bodied men who walk the streets and byways of America seeking work that is denied them. They are not asking for alms or charity. They are members of society, human beings who have a God-given right to expend effort in direct ration to the good life they wish to enjoy. More disconcerting is the fact that they are human beings upon whom other human beings, wives and young children, depend for good and necessities that sustain life.

With the whole nation geared to a war economy, it is difficult to get the full impact of automation on manpower and employment. Congressional investigations, dealing with the replacement of men by machines, present an outlook for future employment that is foreboding. It is estimated that men are being replaced by machines at a rate of 40,000 jobs a week. Knowledgeable men in the field of automation and cybernation completely destroy the myth that automation creates jobs. If that were true, they state, there would be no point in automating! Reputable spokesmen for labor estimate that during the next ten years, 41,000,000 new jobs will be needed to take care of job displacements by automation and the new entrants into the labor market.

What about the farmer? Only fifty years ago, our farmers made up 50 percent of the population. Today they make up only 6 percent. Statistics of the 1960 U.S. Census disclose the whole exodus that is taking place. The farm population in 1950 was 25,000,000 and just ten years later had decreased to 15,000,000. On the 4,000,000 farms then operating, 1,500,000 farms families were striving to eke out an existence on less than $1,500 per year. As this book is being written each year is witnessing a half million people leaving farms. Their fate is inevitable. Unable to procure the modern equipment of the corporate farm, they are driven off their own acres due to their inability to pay taxes and to avoid foreclosures. Technically unskilled, and without savings, they are forced futilely to seek employment in cities where millions are already out of work because of automation.

At a time when thirty million Americans are going to bed each night suffering from lack of proper nourishment, and three quarters of the people of the world await the enjoyment of their first square meal; the nation's approach to the farm problem is both insane and criminal. There is no indictment too harsh for a policy that has permitted billions of dollars of foodstuffs to rot in government storage, that expends billions of dollars each year for letting farmland lie idle, and that callously drives the producer from his land when widespread hunger stalks both this country and the world.

What of our nation's 19,000,000 elderly citizens, those over sixty-years old? Here a nation is ungrateful, callous and unmerciful as to human needs. Statistics bear out that approximately one-half of the elderly are compelled to eke out existences on less than $1,000 per year. Such meager income is not only insufficient to provide food, shelter, clothing and medical needs, but leaves nothing for any of life's enjoyments. Destitute and helpless, these millions of our citizens find little that makes their sunset years either contented or meaningful. Only in death are anguish and heartbreak terminated.

When we come to consider survival in terms of the homes Americans live in, even the most smug and complacent in our society should be appalled. One third, or over 18,000,000, or the 58,000,000 homes in America are listed as unsound, according to the 1960 Census Bureau. More graphically, 13,000,000 units are listed as unfit and dilapidated. And, as with the small farmer, the spectre of over-burdening taxation and indebtedness likewise plagues the home-owner.

Between World War II and 1961 the mortgage debt on homes rose 600 percent to a total figure of $146 billion, with an annual foreclosure rate of 80,000 homes annually. Since 1961 to the present the total mortgage indebtedness on homes has risen to the staggering figure of $295 billion, according to the U.S. Department of Commerce. Never since the Great Depression of the 1930's have so many homes been foreclosed on and additional evictions at even higher rates are the gloomy prospects for the nation's homeowner's.

In considering the over-all public and private indebtedness, we are dealing with figures so astronomical that few people can get the impact of their meaning as related to the individual citizen. Of course, he is somewhat startled to learn that the total debt today is more than double what it was just ten years ago, that currently the debt is rising at an annual rate somewhere around 100 billion dollars. U.S. Department of Commerce figures, estimating up to June 30, 1969, set the total public and private debt at 1.6 trillion dollars. The breakdown shows that over $500,000,000,000 (one-half **trillion** dollars) is owed by families and individuals on home mortgages, installment credit, personal loans and charge accounts.

In listing the Federal debt of only $305 billion, there is no inclusion of the $80 billion government securities held by Federal agencies and trust funds. Nor is there any inclusion of the future Federal commitments that exist. The late Senator Harry Byrd of Virginia as Chairman of the Senate Finance Committee issued a statement in 1963 that the authorizations, debt and other commitments as of July, 1963 totaled $1,242 billion. Figures on what such future commitments are today are not available.

It is realistic to set the total indebtedness, public and private, including the future Federal commitments at a figure exceeding two and a half **trillion** dollars.

Translated into figures that can be comprehended, conservatively using publicly documented figures, we find that every man, woman and child in America is personally in debt for $12,500. For each family of four, the liability of indebtedness totals one-twentieth of a million dollars. Related to the entire nation, the total indebtedness spells out hopeless insolvency and a perpetual threat to individual survival.

It is in light of the foregoing that we come to give thought to the outbreak of crime and violence that signifies the breakdown and rebellion in society. Across the breadth and length of the land, excluding no area of our nation, crime is on the increase. It is increasing faster than the rate of population. In the spring of 1967 the President's "Commission on Law Enforcement and Administration of Justice" released its report on the alarming increase of crime in the nation. While it was disconcerting to learn that the crime wave had increased over 30 percent during the past five years, one particular aspect should have shaken the most complacent and callous in our midst. It was this: **More crimes are committed by 15-year-olds than any other age group.**

We must face the appalling fact that assault, robbery, rape and murder no longer fall in the providence of a hardened criminal element. They are the acts that predominantly of tragically "crossed up" teen-agers. They are the acts of the nation's children, barely out of elementary school, who are brought before the bar of justice to be meted out the nation's severest penalties for having committed the nation's most serious crimes.

We have degenerated to a society that actually spawns criminals!

Not only have the streets of America become unsafe for citizens pursuing their normal errands and business, but no one is secure from attack or violence on his own premises. Every stranger is suspect and more frightening is that the risk of assault from our friends and relatives exceeds that from strangers. When riots are added to the already alarming disregard for person and property, the situation borders on outright anarchy. Moreover, there is no evidence upon which to believe the state of lawlessness will abate or get better.

When one considers the wholesale moral and ethical breakdown that permeates the whole society, both private and public, we are indeed a nation in the throes of debauchment, decay and ultimate destruction.

In the arena of international relationships, we confront the epitome of insecurity and threat to mass survival. Only the irrational are unable to recognize the threat to all life that is posed by the presence of nuclear warheads that can be zeroed-in on every major nuclear striking force that can level every city in the world 125 times, that can obliterate the entire population of Russia and China combined 500 times, and could literally destroy Russia 1250 times. It must be assumed that Russia also possesses such "over-kill" power.

If the nuclear power of the United States alone were converted to an equivalent amount of TNT that was spread evenly over the nation, the entire population would be walking ankle-deep in such explosive material. The thought is soul-chilling.

The devastating potential of nuclear striking power hangs as a Damoclean sword over all mankind. All that is necessary is the pushing of the button marked "Total Annihilation" and the life expectancy of all peoples is automatically reduced to a time span of fifteen minutes. The survival of the world is now dependent on nothing short of a complete dismantling of all nuclear weaponry. The failure to do so, even delay in doing so, can only bear witness to a blackened cinder whirling uninhabited in space.

It will be mute testimony to the temporary insanity of man and the indifference of a people who possessed no dynamic desire to live.

The preceding pages have covered only broadly the existing threats to survival and have highlighted only sketchily the dangerous environment in which mankind struggles to work out its wellbeing. Such coverage has been largely statistical, and statistics are a far cry from considering human beings. There has been no attempt to bare the soul of America, to reveal the inner heartache, the mental anguish, the anxieties, and the despair that are the personal crosses borne by most Americans. However, to the vast majority of our citizens there is no need to dramatize by words, and extended detail, existing hardships and predicaments.

People don't have to be told that they are suffering. They know it through bitter and exacting experience. There is nothing that words can add in portraying hunger to the person who has not sufficient to eat, or in portraying frustration to the person who is futilely seeking employment, or in portraying insecurity to the person who has lost his home, his farm, or his small business. There is nothing that words can add in describing despair and hopelessness to the boy or girl who is a dropout and unable to find a place in society.

If one seeks statistical reports as to the detailed extent of the nation's problems, there are many sources. Volumes are available covering the widespread poverty that plagues the nation. There are magazines and government reports giving statistics to surfeit on the crime wave, on drop-outs from school, on foreclosures, on mental break-down, and the displacement of jobs through automation. Details of every description are available. In fact, one needs only to turn on the radio or TV, or scan the daily newspaper, to be apprised of the increasing insecurity permeating all of society.

"Challenge to Crisis" is not written to make a report on crisis. It is directed to those who are undergoing crisis. It is written for the purpose of showing that it is within the people's hands, and within their own power, to actualize all renovations and all social changes that improve their lot. This book is written that many people may envision a new order amongst men where hunger and hardship are no longer present, where every solitary individual can find meaningful satisfaction living and raising children, and where peace of mind and inspiration are a reality for all human beings.

This book is written not to capture the look of hunger that gnawing stomachs reflect in the eyes of little children. This book is written that needless poverty can be erased from our land, and eventually all lands, so that the aspirations, hopes and natural urges of all boys and girls, irrespective of their race or color, can be bountifully fulfilled.

We are not concerned with portraying the hopelessness of the father who after many tries is unable to find employment, and depicting the desperation that shakes every fibre of his being in seeing his family suffer in consequence of his failure. We are, however, deeply concerned to point a way that affords every father his God-given right to expend effort within an economic framework that provides him and his loved ones with full benefit of his nation's resources and technology.

The book is not written to penetrate into the hearts and minds of the home-owner, the farmer, and the businessman, and feel the emptiness that they feel when foreclosure notices evict them from properties which represent the best part of their lives in work or savings. This book is written that every family will have inviolate ownership of home, secure from any threats of mortgages or liens, and every farmer, businessman and small manufacturer will have a role in the technological economy and cannot be excluded from enjoying his inherent and earned right in the whole productive machinery.

It is not the desolation and helplessness of the men and women over sixty-five, removed from society to fend for themselves on Social Security checks that don't even cover necessities, that we want to emphasize. We want to plead their rightful place in the stream of human life, show gratitude for the contributions they made during working years, and out of the abundance that can be produced make it possible for them to travel, study, pursue hobbies, and enjoy the final years of their lives under no duress, or dependence on others, for all requirements that make life satisfying and meaningful.

When we consider the young boys and girls of this generation, bearing in mind that during this decade over 50 percent of the entire population became under twenty-five years old, it is difficult simply to draw a contrast. Yet, it is not the protest, the frustrations, the despair, the motivations to violence, the indifference to learning that we want to highlight. It is the blue-printing of a New Order in social structure within which every youngster has the fullest opportunity to educate himself, and to assume a role in society which constantly encourages him to perform to excellence.

We as a nation of 200,000,000 Americans have strayed far afield in working out human relationships, in shaping our lives and fulfilling our destinies. Belatedly, we must ask ourselves where we have erred in our ways of living and dealing with each other. What are the basic causes that have led to an era of inequities, lawlessness, and the inability for millions to find work, and the deplorable struggle of even greater numbers to provide for the basic necessities of life? Does plenty mean want? Why should children cry for food when there is too much? Who is responsible for the "planned scarcity" that underlies our whole approach to production?

Do we have the boldness to ask: What groups, what institutions, what set of rules or laws, or what set of circumstances restrain a nation from employing all its manpower, all its resources, and all its science in providing to abundance for all the needs of all the people? At whose direction, or in whose interest, are acres upon acres of productive farm land forced into idleness, half of our machine capacity is consigned to a state of non-operation, and engineered technology needlessly detained on the nation's drawingboards?

Do we have the courage to ask: To whom is the colossal indebtedness owed of over two trillion dollars? To whom goes the interest on this unpayable lien against man's future, and that of unborn generations? To whom goes the tangible assets when claims go unpaid and foreclosers demand their pound of flesh? More pointedly: How has a nation of 200,000,000 people, which possessed its own resources and supplied all its own manpower, and contained within its own boundaries the technology to turn raw materials into an abundance of usable goods, become insolvent and hopelessly indebted to entities that contributed nothing tangible to production?

Above all, do we have the sensitivity to life itself to ask: In whose interest are our best manhood sacrificed and the nation's resources wasted in periodic wars? Is peace denied mankind because the function of war, with all its attendant brutality and human suffering, are mandatory stabilizers of our private capitalistic economy?

These are the questions that must be asked by a people who genuinely desire freedom and liberation from involuntary servitude. Our environment becomes increasingly dangerous and prolonged indifference by a suffering people can only spell disaster. Failure to put our own house in order provides the fertile soil for anarchy and rapine, and foredooms a world to nuclear obliteration.

There are answers to all the basic questions we have posed. There are solutions to all the basic problems that afflict mankind. There is a way to peace, to an abundant life for all peoples, to a fulfillment of youth's noblest visions and of age's longheld dreams.

All that is required is faith in ourselves, the courage to weigh intelligently the nation's plight, and the determination to endorse and adopt remedial measures.

Chapter 1

APATHY AND REBELLION

T O THE AVERAGE person and consideration to do anything constructive about the nation's problems appears beyond his capability. Any contemplation of the hour-to-hour threat of hydrogen bombs descending from the sky is beyond his comprehension. So he reasons, or fails to apply reason, in both ignorance and futility. He immediately shies away from anyone audacious enough even to raise the subjects for discussion. However, for such disinterest he should not be decried or ridiculed.

Only compassion and understanding can be felt for such indifference on the part of so many people. Further, the person who dares call his soul his own, who views no institution or system of economies and government as so "sacred" that it is immune from honest analysis, knows in his heart that the vast majority of people really do care about the survival and well-being of both themselves and their loved ones. It is only a question of not knowing what to think and what to do. They are at a loss as to just how their lot could be improved in a very insecure and disturbing society.

More seriously, the people have come to learn, often through bitter experience, that they live in a society in which the freedom of ideas extends largely to the right of agreeing and not to the right of disagreeing. There is a penalty for questioning established "systems," established "institutions" and the status quo throughout society. And how are such penalties administered? And by whom are they assessed?

They are administered and assessed by those very institutions and privileged groups which are the chief beneficiaries of the status quo in conducting the business of the nation. In progressively decreasing influence, the force to make people conform stems from the "establishments" on the highest levels of industry, finance and government, down by those existing on local levels. There is not a byway or corner in America that the tentacles for silencing all non-conformists do not reach. Every pressure and intimidation are used to choke and suppress all rational and imaginative thinking. Conform or suffer consequences is the only choice given to the people. No one is excluded. The ramifications and interlocking relationships of our whole economic, financial and political structures make every citizen vulnerable. This is the inevitable result of powerblocs gaining despotic power by planned scarcity, planned economic structures, planned mass indebtedness, and planned "hot" and "cold" wars. None of them have been God-ordained, nor prompted by natural causes. It is assuredly understandable when the worker refrains from caustic criticism of flagrant injustices prevalent in the price-fixing of monopolistic cartels, because such voiced reactions could jeopardize his employment. It is equally understandable when no one, whether he be small businessman, farmer, or just ordinary consumer, shows open antagonism toward any aspect of the whole privately controlled banking structure, because no person can survive economically without such institutions carrying his loan, his mortgage or his time-payments. There are serious penalties for not kowtowing and bending to those who wield the economic whiplash.

What tugs at the heartstrings, and fires every atom in one's body to red-hot indignation, is to observe the most peonized and destitute in our midst forced to suffer in silence lest they be cut off from the alms tossed at their feet. Here we have the elderly on social security, the jobless who receive unemployment checks, the small pensioner, and those whose only means with which to stave off death are government "commodities" and the welfare check. What tragedy, what irony that liberty should be exchanged for such pittance when so many tens of thousands of Americans have given their lives for the avowed purpose of preserving it!

Conformity, premised on duress and reprisals, leads to the more serious conditions of indifference and apathy. A people made to fetch and carry too long, solely in the interest and for the exclusive benefit of financial overseers, become as Pavlov's dogs with no intelligent will of their own. Not only does the individual move and act according to the whims and dictates of those who direct the nation, but the whole citizenry responds en masse, politically and militarily, when the "shot is called."

The conditioning and subjugation that have taken place are not difficult to understand. The process for subduing and enslaving a people is very simple of formula. It is worked in two directions. It is two-fold in execution. Intimidate, reject and penalize the vast majority so that they have no alternative to conforming. At the same time, to a sprinkling on every level, give advantages, bonuses and status symbols so that they too will not oppose the "system" but in fact will serve as a buffer, protecting the autocratic policymakers at the top.

In the broadest skeleton form, this is what has happened to America. By the time you finish this book, much detail will have been filled in, and the basic pieces of the national jigsaw puzzle put in place so that you can grasp not only what has befallen an unsuspecting people but you can also envision what can be done to raise the nation and all its citizens onto a plateau of performing where institutions serve man instead of enslave him. You will foresee a future where human relationships are predicated on the brotherhood of man, and where the inherent good in every individual finds expression, not his beastliness.

This book will deal with three Americas. There is the America that people **think** they live in. There is the America that they **do** live in. And there is the America that they **could** live in. As you read the ensuing pages of this book, distinct lines of demarcation will begin to appear, separating each of these three Americas.

The Twin Reactions to Oppression

Right now we must concern ourselves, not so much with the injustices and wrongs making up our society, but more with the state of mind of our people and their mass indifference to their own well-being and survival. At the same time those who wish to analyze the times correctly, and what they portend, must fully appreciate and understand the rebellion that is erupting throughout all of society. Let us make no mistake in recognizing that both apathy and rebellion are the twin reactions to extended oppression. They are the distinct, yet inseparable, effects stemming from causes that persist in suppressing the natural rights and urges of the people.

Rebellion has no origin in the minds of people who enjoy security and derive satisfaction as participants in society. Rebellion arises in those areas of a society where oppression exacts its most severe toll, where human beings are subjected to the most degrading existence, and where basic human rights are the most flagrantly denied. Man rebels against that which restrains his performing and that which openly threatens his survival.

This is the circumstance that underlies the whole Civil Rights movement, the Negro revolution. It is unfortunate that such rebellion should demonstrate itself in the form of violence, blood in the street and injury to both persons and property. It is even more unfortunate that it should result in increased ill-feeling between races. But it is not the race riots, the defiance of the policeman trying to maintain order, the wild gun shots, and the killing of the innocent bystander that must be indicted. These are the inevitable results, however lamented, that stem from causes much, much deeper. It is the oppression itself that must be condemned. It is the social environment, compelling such degradation of human beings, which must be brought before an unprejudiced bar of justice.

A hundred years have passed since the signing of the Emancipation Proclamation. Yet today overwhelming numbers of the 22,000,000 Negroes in this country find themselves isolated in the slum areas of the nation's cities or in the rural southland. To date they have been given only "paper" rights and are treated, by any standard, as second-rate citizens. The heart sickens at the sight of the rat-infested, squalid tenements, the deplorable living conditions making up the Harlems and the racial ghettoes throughout the nation. Denied the opportunity for education, the Negro is condemned for his bad manners and lack of social consciousness. Denied the opportunity for work, the Negro is condemned for being unclean and unkempt. And the most warped of reasoning is the condemnation of his revolt when oppression becomes unbearable.

The time will come, when evolutionary social change is viewed in retrospect, and the American Negro will be acclaimed for having made the first bold step in challenging the gross malfunctioning of our society. The fact that his rights were those most greatly suppressed should not detract from the contribution rendered. He at the same time had the lesser tools with which to wage battle.

Crime

By no means, however, is the Negro revolt the only area of rebellion to restraint and oppression. It is only more readily identified as to direction and purpose. The whole spectrum of crime, when analyzed basically, is a rebellion against society, a violent protest against circumscriptions that prevent constructive participation in day-to-day living. No more soul-searing realization can come to anyone of us than the inescapable fact that we live within an economic, political and social environment that encourages or forces people into crime.

As a nation we have failed to provide an environment within which all Americans, irrespective of race or color, can find full employment, own their homes, educate their children, and live decently and wholesomely. Millions or men, willing to work, cannot be denied work and then tens of thousands of them not be expected to steal that which they lack wages to purchase. Thirty millions of our citizens cannot be compelled to live in poverty, without adequate food, housing and medical care and then a large segment in sheer desperation not be expected to wrest from others, by gun if necessary, that which the nation could produce to abundance.

Even more seriously, a nation cannot be witness to millions of its boys and girls dropping out of school, show an inability to give them adequate employment, glorify crime and violence on TV, radio and newsstand, and then expect that tens of thousands will not be moved to commit crimes in tempo with an economic arrangement where the spoils always go to the strong.

Murder? Here society must bear mankind's harshest indictment. No nation, or society, can draft an eighteen-year-old boy into the armed forces, indoctrinate him with the justification for killing to protect his rights, return him to a civilian life where those rights are denied, and then expect that such "killer" training will be automatically erased. Nor can a society so restrict a man's ability to work and provide for the needs of the human body that life itself is threatened, and then expect that man will not take another's life that his own might be preserved.

People are not bad by nature. It has been an irrational society that has produced irrational conduct. We shall come to understand that the crimes of our institutions against mass humanity dwarf in magnitude the crimes of person against person. We shall further come to understand that they are responsible for breeding the very callousness, aberration or desperation which causes individual crime to flourish.

Intellectual Revolt

There is another form of rebellion taking place that must be noted. It might be rightfully termed an intellectual revolt because it is made up of persons who have achieved, or could achieve status in the "system" but find the inequities so repugnant that they are moved to rebel openly.

There will be no attempt here to set down a listing of men, writings or movements which make up the intellectual revolt of this generation. It would be difficult to evaluate the relative importance of each as to its contribution to the over-all social change that is now gestating. However, we would be seriously remiss if we did not make special mention of the revolt on America's campuses.

For years the colleges and universities of this nation were primarily attended by those who were only interested in becoming "trained" to fill the highest positions in industry and business or in the professions and government. They were generally the offspring of the wealthier who went to college as a matter of course and were oriented to the thinking of the "successful."

Gradually, commencing with the GI Bill after World War II, the college student bodies became interspersed with those coming from all strata of society. Opportunities to go to college increased greatly with scholarships, government loans, grants and the recognition that a high school diploma no longer insured employment.

The Civil Rights movement entered the scene jolt the conscience of the young people that there was an idealistic America and there was an America that betrayed and belied our oft-voiced idealism. At the same time, the hidden America of the poor and destitute came into focus. Together, these two submerged blights of the nation awakened the conscience of the young on the campuses.

Adult America, too deadened in spirit, awakened only statistically. The young's response was different. They responded in spirit, a communion of minds and souls, genuinely concerned about their fellow human beings who were sorely in need of surcease from intolerable oppression.

But it was involvement in the brutal and undefined war in Vietnam and the conversion of the nation into a military state with all the insanity of "over-kill," the stockpiling of nuclear warheads, nerve gas and biological weapons that made the young rebel openly.

Today there are 6,700,000 young men and women on American campuses. As yet is displaying open rebellion against the injustices and false values of our society, the entire enrollment constitutes the one potential force in our nation that is large enough to encompass the whole society in seeking total renovation. They are the only force that in uncommitted to any group and which is not yet molded into the system, and thus vulnerable to economic intimidation.

By Their Own Bootstraps

Assuredly, the nation is not without intellectual capability, both adult and young, to solve its problems. As yet there has not appeared, however, any approach to the people themselves, especially the nation's destitute and the young men and women preparing for advent into society, that they might be given premises and yardsticks upon which and by which to pass judgment on existing wrongs and proffered innovations for their enhancement and participation in society.

It is this vacuum that this book would endeavor to fill with compelling considerations.

The folly of the past has been that the people have relied on institutions, as institutions, and on the privileged in their midst, to better conditions. The people have failed to realize that the whole economy and the financial structure were predicated on the insecurity of the many that the few might have over-security. Naively they have accepted the false promises that an end to their suffering was imminent, and that they should be admonishment that to seek immediate social reform smacked of revolution.

Little the people have known how all the cards were stacked against them. Blindly they moved at the behest of predatory and monopolistic forces in society that have had no real sensitivity toward human life or regard for the stability of the nation. It was inevitable that mass impoverishment should befall the people, that larger and larger segments would be excluded from participation, and that financial bondage should fetter the whole citizenry. But more tragic was the bankruptcy of character which sapped the people's will to fight back. It became easier to acquiesce than protest, to conform than suffer penalties.

The author of this book is under no illusion that there is any finality to what is presented nor is he egotistical enough to believe that in most instances all will be stated as clearly or adequately as the subject merits. Much will remain unsaid. Much could have been better stated by others. Unequivocally, however, this book is not written for the protection of institutions that have subordinated the importance of human beings. It is an attempt to give people an insight into their individual importance, restore ballast to their thinking, and chart a course of cooperative action for a new birth of freedom for all people.

Chapter 2

BALLAST IN OUR THINKING

W E WANT to address, and to appeal to, all strata of our society, including the most privileged, even those who wield abnormal power, and endeavor to reason together. Our environment becomes increasingly dangerous with each day that passes and overlong delay in solving our problems can only spell disaster for all mankind.

There is no magic formula by which one can arouse people from their apathy and indifference to a cruel reality. There is no mystical command that can still the voices and acts of misdirected rebellion. Nor are admonishments of citizenship responsibilities, and patriotic exhortations in the name of liberty the answer. Into the minds and hearts of Americans must come reasoning, and understanding, upon which to transform apathy into hope and faith, to channel rebellion toward constructive goals attainable, and to rekindle a genuine desire on the part of every individual to live and participate in a meaningful society.

The need of the hour is to identify each and every individual with his environment. More to the point, man must be identified with himself. A clarion call must ring out across the nation that will reach the ear of every living America. Its message must penetrate into every home, into the areas of deepest degradation, and exclude no one, irrespective of impoverishment or condition of servitude. And that message should be simply this—

Awaken, ye greatly wronged people! Awaken to the realization that you are the arbiters of your own lives and your own destinies. We know that you wish a better life for yourselves, and your children, but you know not how to seek it. Therefore you bear your lot in silence. Harken, for we come to show you that the injustices that afflict you are man-made afflictions. We come to show you that the problems that burden you are artificially created burdens. Most importantly, we come to point a way so that those afflictions can be erased and those burdens can be lifted.

We understand that you initial reaction to what we offer may be one of mistrust and misgiving. Your past has been filled with empty promises and broken pledges. But we come not as politicians seeking office, nor as those posing as saviors for a price. We have no promises to offer or pledges to make. We come only to accentuate your own importance, your own strength, that you may affect your own deliverance.

There is much that we want to tell you about the financial institutions that have placed a whole nation in bondage. There is much that we want to reveal to you as to how our economic structure functions, impoverishing millions while a surfeit of food rots in storehouses and millions of acres of fertile soil lie idle. There is much that we want to uncover for you as to how political strategists move you as pawns on a rigged chessboard. There is also much about which to enlighten you as to why there is such criminal waste of manpower, resources and science when so much work goes undone in our nation. But all this must come later.

Our concern now is that you may be given ballast in your thinking that you feel a new sense of being and get the first glimpses of what this nation could be when all human relationships are premised on the equal inherent rights of every individual.

Let us quickly and briefly consider the cardinal premises upon which all that follows must be your consciousness make them part of your constant thinking, and you are well on the road to your liberation.

The first premise is that **we live in a good universe, one that is balanced and rational.** All that we observe in nature operates according to the patterns and cycles conforming to laws that can be coded. Our increased observation only further bears out that we have an overall orderly framework within which to postulate and work out the rational behavior of man. For our purpose, there will be no need to grasp an academic understanding of the physical sciences. Nor will there be any need to perceive scientifically the immensity of a galaxy or the minuteness of an atom.

We must simply understand that all men are born into this world, occupy an impartial planet lush with resources, and are left to work out their existence. None come into life with anything. None leave life with anything. Everything is here for man's use and betterment only during each person's span of mortal existence.

Since we are dealing with literal human beings, ordinary two-legged creatures, striving, aspiring and exerting themselves on this three-dimensional planet, there must be agreed-upon rules for human conduct. The behavior of one individual has a bearing on each and every other individual. Right here enters the need for laws, social structure and government. Right here we must seek common denominators for living together, working together, playing together and learning together.

The second premise is that **every human being is important.** There is no exception to this inherent status of every man, woman or child, irrespective of race or color, irrespective of mental or physical capability, irrespective of riches or poverty. The right to partake of God's bounty, the right to develop one's innate talents to the utmost, do not come from men or from institutions. These rights originate with each human being himself with his advent into life. They are the rights he is endowed with by an impartial Creator that has made all life possible.

Let no human being permit any other human being to convince him otherwise. To do so would be to deny one's own birthright!

The third premise is that **human beings are of paramount importance.** Everything else is secondary. Tools, technology, social structure, and government, have no purposeful end-result in themselves. Their worth, their usefulness, forever and always must be judged in direct ratio to their enhancement and improvement of people as human beings.

Man was not meant for systems and institutions. Systems and institutions were meant for man.

The fourth premise is that **the supreme power rests constantly with the people.** In the people's hands is the inviolate power to affect every change that leads to their betterment. There is no change, socially, economically, or politically that they cannot bring to pass. There is none to stay their hand. A people need not suffer inequity or hardship one moment longer than the point at which they understand what change should be embraced.

*   *   *   *

It is hoped that you have grasped the fundamental significance of the fore going premises. They are not theoretical rules of a school book. They are the inescapable premises underlying human relationships. It has been the merciless and ruthless violation of these premises that has led to the suffering of so many people. It is their arbitrary violation that has led to the plight of the nation and the world.

Awaken, fellow beings, to the fact that all our problems are man-made. And as man-made problems, they are all solvable. It is in the interest of greedy and power-hungry men and the institutions they control that millions of you, and your children, must suffer needlessly.

Gird up your loins! Assume the importance and the strength that is yours. Let us act with one voice and with one purpose to restore our nation to the saneness and justice in all its functionings. Let us shape a future where every child, be he black, yellow, red or white, can take on individual significance and achieve personal distinction.

There is more than enough in this nation for all its people. Let us arise from our apathy and our confusion; let us focus our rebellion and direct our efforts into constructive channels leading to the reality of a better tomorrow.

A beneficent Creator has entrusted us to shape our own destinies.

Chapter 3

YOUR STAKE IN A BOUNTIFUL UNIVERSE

T HE FIRST PREMISE that was stated dealt with observable conclusion that we live in a good Universe, one that is balanced and rational. To many this premise will shape up as a mere platitude and not deserving of much attention. Yet it is of vast importance. This is the most basic of basic frameworks in which to consider man and all his functions. It is here that man stakes his first claim, the right of equal opportunity to partake of that which Nature herself provides bountifully.

The perspective which we must have is that each person comes into life without anything and he leaves without anything. He doesn't come equipped with clothes, a lunch bucket, a tent, or any mode of transportation. All needs must be met after his arrival. Multiplying the individual by hundreds of millions doesn't alter the fact that human life enters onto the earthly stage and finds all raw ingredients already present out of which to fashion his needs, his comforts, and to insure his survival. Whether we identify such raw stock as soil, as trees, as ore, as water, or as all the atoms on the physicist's periodic chart, it was all here before man arrived. Even all forms of electric magnetic energy, not excluding atomic fission and the ultimate harnessing of energy through fusion, were potentially here when the cavemen chipped the first flint-stone and stood agasp at the spark of energy he had released.

The whole process of natural growth was not a man-made process. It, too, was here before man made his appearance. Even should the chemist duplicate plant life, photo-synthesis, in his laboratory, it will still be employing the raw ingredients of nature. Whether we consider organic matter, animal and vegetable life, or whether we consider the inorganic matter of inanimate material, we are dealing with the same atoms and electrons that compose the whole physical universe. These are the universal building-blocks that Nature herself has provided, in unlimited abundance, for man's use.

The point we are getting at is simply this: The raw ingredients of nature, the universal building-blocks making up this earth and all that surrounds it, are the inherent property of all human beings. There is no Celestial Plaque that stipulates that only a few shall partake of the raw stock that abounds so plentifully over the whole planet. There is no Divine Will and Last Testament that parcels out a larger share to some and a pittance to others. There is no Olympian Keeper of the Gate who arbitrarily rules that you cannot gain access if your skin is of the wrong color, your nationality different, or your religious views at variance with the majority.

Every person now living, and every child yet to be born, has a God-given right to have equal access to Nature's storehouse. At the same time, he should have equal opportunity to expend human effort toward refining all raw ingredients into finished products. No person, or group of persons, or institution, has a right to build fences and preclude the preponderance of human beings from enjoying the natural resources put here by the Creator. Nor does the right exist for such corralled wealth to be passed on to privileged persons, or groups, of the next generation, thus perpetuating and compounding the injustice to humanity.

All human beings, excluding no one, have an equal title to the surfeit of resources that abound on this planet, including the inexhaustible potential of energy found in nature. Every person has such stake in the material and energy makeup of this world simply because he is born. It is his inherent prerogative to partake thereof during the fullspan of his mortal existence. Only at death are his claims relinquished.

Accumulated Knowledge—Legacy of All People

The same holds equally true in respect to all the contributions that all mankind have made to all knowledge up the many centuries. Such contributions are not the exclusive knowledge of the few to enhance only their own well-being and survival. All achievements, and all advancements, up the corridor of time in physics, in chemistry, in transportation, in communication, in the techniques of production, in medicine, are the legacy of all the people. Every newborn child is the rightful heir to all knowledge accumulated since man first set foot on terra firma.

It is immaterial whether you have, or do not have, a scientific grasp of what the Galileos, the Keplers, and the Newtons contributed to the first understanding of heavenly bodies and the forces of nature. It is not necessary that you understand what the James Watts contributed to the first complication of power of machines, what the Marconis, the Faradays, the Maxwells and the Edisons contributed to an understanding and application of electricity. Nor do you have to grasp the exhaustive and painstaking research and experimentation that encompasses all the contributions of the Bohrs, the Daltons, the Einsteins, and the Enrico Fermis from the first detection of atomic structure up to the present harnessing of nuclear power.

There would be no end to our listings if we were to cover the contributions of the first alphabet, the first offerings in mathematics, the first steps in metallurgy, the first crude machines of farm, of factory and of transportation, the first movable type and steps toward wireless communication, the first discoveries in medicine, and the firsts in every existing field of human endeavor, and then trace them to the present. Included would have to be the billions of people themselves who have inhabited the planet. Without their contributions, however menial, all achievements in science, technology, and in the clearing, the cultivating and the building of the world would have been impossible.

The important point is that each person now living has a stake in all that learned men have contributed to and sacrificed for up the centuries. No person, or group of persons, has any priority on the vast accumulation of knowledge any more than they have on all natural resources. Our present know-how is but an extension of all the genius and labor that preceded those living today. All such past contributions are willed to all mankind.

When we come to consider the workings of our present economy, its institutions and existing human arrangements, we will understand graphically why we have millions destitute, unemployed, millions sick without medical care, and equal numbers breaking mentally under the stresses and demands of mere existence. It will not be difficult to realize how they have been shortsuited of any inheritance in our vast resources and our reservoir of accumulated wisdom.

Rational, Lush, and Impartial Universe

Unreservedly, we are the inhabitants of a good Universe. It is not only lush with raw ingredients, and abounding in unlimited energy, but it is impartial as to whom it shall benefit. There are no decreed favorites. Onto this prolific orb, whirling in balanced pattern, the Creator has placed man to work out his destinies, endowing him also with the creative capability to construct better and better tools by which to transform a primitive existence into a highly technical and cultured civilization. In the evolutionary process of material progress, man was left to work out his relationships of brother to brother.

That he has worked out human relationships badly, and unjustly, and irrationally, is no fault of the Creator or the handiwork demonstrated in Nature. Every display, from the most minute particles in the nucleus of an atom to the most remote galaxies, billions of light-years removed, accentuates rationality and balance. The seasonal cycle, the oxygen-carbon dioxide cycle of plant life, the actions and reactions, the causes and effects of all the forces engaged in the interplay of the Universe bear out the functioning of a Celestial Arrangement that came into being and exists with determinable and measurable pattern.

Scientists are now discovering that the same radioactive rays emanating from the nuclei of atoms are emanating from outer space, substantiating the conclusion that the most basic common denominators of all matter are universal. Perhaps even more intriguing is the fact that man is positioned essentially midway in relative size between the smallest particles we can measure and our farthest outreaches into space.

Man is the hub of his own existence.

It is from this central station of all creation that man must work out his needs, his comforts, and his aspirations. That he has the capability to be rational, that he has a motivation for humanness, there can no question. Man will embrace that which is constructive, that which is just, and that which is ethical if he is given the chance to express his true self freely.

Currently, power-blocs, predatory interests and abnormal human relationships have alienated man from himself. However, even such alienation has its extreme limits. Men and nations can be denied free and natural expression to a certain degree of circumscription and oppression. Then they will rebel and demand recognition of inherent rights together with the opportunity to live in rational relationship with each other.

Emblazoned across the sky is the Creator's admonition and penalty for irrational behavior: Misuse my bounty and all-pervading wisdom so that hundreds of millions of my children have to suffer needless want in both body and spirit and you shall reap anarchy! Misuse my unlimited energy in war instead of peace, and shall reap obliteration!

People have become estranged from Nature. They have lost their identity with and Infinite Universe of which they are an integral part. However, it is not a material relationship that must be renewed as we would consider carloads of grain from fields of fertile soil, or tons of ore from mines, or even atomic plants that extract energy from radioactive materials. Nor is it mathematical in scope as we would measure our relative size, or as we would pinpoint our location in the vastness of space.

It includes all of these but is considerably more. We have lost reverence for life, and with it we have lost a sense of being wanted, of being needed, of being important, of belonging. We don't feel in tune with the throbbing, exuberant, vibrant Universe that gives forth with such myriads of lifeforms, all having a common creation with ourselves. We don't sense that all life, in whatever size and shape, is also a pattern of atoms enhousing a breath of divinity that gives it identity and importance.

We have lost our kinship with Nature.

It is little wonder that we show such callous disregard for ourselves and for our planet. We are indifferent to the pollution of our air by both atomic fall-out and a thousand and one poisonous fumes that contaminate it. We are indifferent to the pollution of our lakes and streams by industrial waste and by indiscriminate use of insecticides that destroy the delicate balance between plant and animal life.

We have become indifferent to brutal and immoral wars that needlessly maim and kill millions of our fellow beings.

The net result is that we have lost reverences for our individual bodies and spirits. Instead of recognizing our individual importance and embracing a good Universe, we seek every avenue of escape from the rigors of reality without even trying to understand the causes of our problems. We pour billions of dollars' worth of alcohol into our bodies that we may numb our senses and hide from our responsibilities. We drug our whole bloodstream with a constant avalanche of sedatives from aspirin to morphine that we may avoid facing up to actualities. And if such weren't enough, we recklessly engage in promiscuity so that venereal diseases can sap the last ounce of vitality from dissipated bodies and can destroy the last incentive of mind and spirit to exert themselves.

The foregoing does not, of course, include all our people, but such moral decay does permeate our whole society. What is alarming is the fact that it is on the increase, and that it involves literally millions of the nation's young boys and girls. Drunkards, drug addicts and syphilitics have little to offer the nation in working out its destiny. They have nothing to offer themselves.

By no means, however, is everything lost and irretrievable. Spirit is indomitable and indestructible. We don't have to wander aimlessly as nomads without anchor points and without purpose. We can regain a positive identity with our Universe, our fellow beings and ourselves. We can rekindle a finer reverence for all life, and we can expand our awareness to an inner realization that each of us reflects the whole of Creation.

Such rebirth of spirit, however, cannot be legislated. It cannot be presented as a gift. It can only come through an understanding of ourselves and of the Universe we inhabit. It can only by first recognizing and accepting the natural rights of every human being—the right of every individual to equal opportunity in the whole life process.

Chapter 4

EVERY HUMAN BEING IS IMPORTANT

THE MOST difficult aspect of presenting the equal importance of every solitary individual that is born onto this planet is in getting people to lift themselves momentarily out of the current grind and confusion of living and get a pristine comprehension of their role in the dram of life. Each of us is so bogged down with the demands of the day, and our interlocking relations with each other, that it becomes nearly impossible to find that moment of solitude in which to weigh our own significance from the vantage point of the Architect of all Creation. Only in so doing, however, can perspective be ours in working out all human relationships successfully.

Up to this point we have stressed the bedrock premise that we are the occupants of a Good Universe that abounds in unlimited resources both in raw stock and energy, that belongs to all people. We have postulated the right of all human beings to benefit from all the knowledge that has accumulated up the centuries. Briefly we have emphasized that no person, or group of persons, or any economic arrangement could justly preclude the preponderance of people from benefiting from either right. Both are inviolate heritage of all peoples.

It is with this fundamental background in mind that we want to consider the individual person and nail down the natural or inalienable rights that are his as a human being. The significance of this consideration cannot be minimized. We are not now concerning ourselves with literal rules, laws, social structures or forms of government. We are concerning ourselves with the rights a person is born with when he first enters life. Only as we comprehend these rights can we evaluate and pass judgment on existing economic and political structures, and the laws and institutions governing man's movements.

It must become indelibly inscribed on the minds and spirits of all people that no rights come from men or institutions. Men and institutions can only interpret them. As such interpretation is done badly; the people needlessly endure hardship, inequity and restraints on both mind and spirit. Conversely, as such interpretation is done intelligently, freedom, material plenty and enhancement of the individual are rewards of all people. Equally imbedded in the consciousness of all must be the adamant fact that no person enters into life with rights that are greater, or are less, than those of any other person. The Creator specified no favorites.

Every person born into existence has an inherent right to live and perform with the same opportunities as each and every human being.

History is replete with men who have stood forth in times of great stress or oppression to thrust high the torch of individual freedom. Amidst confusion and the arbitrary dictates of power-blocs of the day, they rose to light anew the flame of man's cosmic makeup. With few exceptions, such enunciators of human rights were mercilessly persecuted, made to flee to save their lives, and too often were imprisoned, hanged, burned or crucified. The irony of their fate lay in the circumstance that the mass of the people, for whom they had such compassion and genuine concern, did so little to uphold their hands. Then, as now, it was easier, and much safer, to succumb than to defend one's own birthright.

No, history has not been without courageous men defining and enunciating the inborn rights of individuals as human beings. The writers of the Declaration of Independence did so in unmistakable language when they set down:

> We hold these truths to be self-evident: That all men are created equal; that they are endowed by their Creator with certain inalienable rights; that among

these are life, liberty and the pursuit of happiness; that, to secure these rights, governments are instituted among men, deriving their just powers from the consent of the governed.

Every schoolchild has read these lines. Most adults are familiar with them. Few are the persons who truly grasp their import or encompass their intrinsic meaning in practical application.

From the time when Jesus walked the shores of Galilee, preaching, "Inasmuch as ye have done it unto of the least of these my brethren, ye have done it unto me," through the signing of the Declaration, up into modern times, the forerunners of social change have all proclaimed the God-given rights of human beings. They endeavored to translate the inborn rights of each person to person with equal opportunity with the then-existing environment. One is awestruck at the consistency with which these rights have been pleaded.

The prime difficulty in appreciating their significance is our inability to isolate the "rights of man" from the literal conditions existing. Too often we confuse them with statues and regulations and governmental documents or constitutions themselves. This is not to say that these formal stipulations do not at times reflect the basic rights of man. It is saying, however, that whether they do or don't, does not alter the existence of human rights which are constantly and perpetually entitled to expression.

Another difficulty in appreciating the writings of social reformers of the past in their pleading for man's natural rights is that we read their offerings not in the context of the times relating to the physical and scientific limitations during a particular span of history. All advocates of human rights, whether in the area of economic adjustment or in such causes in light of the then-prevailing scientific knowledge and the means of production. It is also necessary to bear in mind the tremendous obstacles to communication which have always existed until the last handful of years. All these factors have had a bearing on the scope of human functioning.

To understand the writings of John Locke and Jean Jacques Rousseau, writing in the 17th and 18th centuries, is to understand the age of feudalism, the crude productive facilities and the theory of "the divine right of kings" that held sway. In the same light, we have to consider the Paines, the Jeffersons and the Washingtons, so prominent in our own history. Their writings, too, must be considered in the context of the virgin territory that existed, the forests that had to be cleared, the land that had to be cultivated, the crude means of production and manufacture, the struggle for independence, and the financial-property interests that were able to exert disproportionate influence.

As we come to consider our current times of explosive knowledge and expanding science, of automated production where the productivity per man has increased a thousand-fold, of instant communication available in every home, and of accelerated transportation spanning the world in hours, we find an entirely different framework within which to consider human rights. Yet the rights are the same. **Only the potential scope of their exercise has become wider.**

Let us get it clear in our thinking that every human being is born with the same inalienable rights as any other human being. Neither man, nor institution, nor laws, nor government can ignore or destroy them. These rights are the endowment of a Beneficent Creator which has shown no partiality by divine circumscription. All circumscriptions are man-made. The same holds true for any contention by any group or race that they are divinely commissioned to lord it over other groups or races. No matter if it be the Jews as God's Chosen, or if it be the Black Muslims, or the White supremists, or the Catholics, or Protestants, or Republicans, or Democrats, or any conceivable group yet created, there is no validity to such contention.

Man was placed on this planet to work out his relationships with his fellow beings so that each individual, irrespective of race or color of skin, had equal opportunity to exercise inalienable rights. Performance alone—not pre-supposed or self-determined superiority nor deliberate conniving—is the only yardstick which should, and can, determine individual worth.

Bearing in mind that we are considering the rights a man is born with, rights that are his regardless of the span of history in which he is considered, let us set them down for all our future analysis respecting our ways of living together, the wrongness of existing economic and political arrangements, and what renovations must be embraced to eradicate inequities and suffering from our land.

All these rights will take on more literal and specific meaning as we translate them into the day-to-day functioning of our society.

Every Human Being's Right to Life

This is the most encompassing inherent right of every person because it transverses the whole spectrum of existence. It deals with the protection and with the preservation of life itself. No organized society can lay claim to being civilized, and in accord with nature, that denies just one of its citizens sufficient food to sustain life along with the water he drinks and the air he breathes. Simply to provide protection from outward physical attack is fulfilling only one-half the obligation of society. The greater responsibility lies in protecting him from starvation by providing equal opportunity to share in the nation's productive potential, or in the case of physical inability to work, the right to share simply because he is a human being. Later we shall consider the right to expend effort, which involves the right to work to provide the maximum comforts of life, but this guarantee is in addition to the basic right of sustaining life.

The paramount motivation of mankind must be reverence for life itself. Only as mankind recognizes that each and every life has an inherent right to full existence, to be terminated only by natural causes, can there be any solid premise upon which to work out mutual responsibilities and benefits.

It is in terms of the infant, invited into this world through the procreational process of its parents, that we can more readily grasp the momentous import of this right to life. Here we confront life in its purest and humblest beginning. It awaits what care, what nurturing, what love society is willing to give it. It is helpless to provide or fulfill any of its many needs. By what reasoning, pray, by what claim to any degree of spiritual motivation, can any society decree that this child is not entitled to exactly the same amount of nourishing food as any other child? By what yardstick is it ruled that one human is important and another's isn't?

But it isn't just food. Does not the same question present itself respecting clothes, shelter, the opportunity to play, and the advantages of good moral and cultural surroundings? Why should one child be shortsuited in contrast to another? And what about a child's right to equal education during its formative years? And the more serious question of equal when sick or injured? How can we escape the challenging postulate that it is the responsibility of society to insure every child equal protection of life? Certainly, when a child has no means by which to fend for itself, its right to live and grow transcends parental ability.

Society can learn a moving lesson by simply observing the average family unit. It would do well to emulate what transpires. Can anyone conceive of a father discriminating against any one of his children because of age, physical or mental prowess, or color of complexion? He knows that every child has an equal right to live. When the table is amply laden with food, he makes no arbitrary ruling that one can partake of all its desires just a limited amount, and still another no food at all. In the case of sickness, or need of medical care, no father, unless he be of twisted mind, would weigh the importance of child over another in determining for whom he should call the doctor.

Instinctively, every parent knows that each child has an equal right to life. Spontaneously, they act to sustain and preserve it.

Now it is a foregone conclusion that no father can provide for his children beyond capacity and productive potential. The same, of course, obtains for society. However, it is the constructive perspective and motivation of the father in recognizing the right of every child to life that is of importance. It is this display of genuine altruism that society as the breadwinner of all the nation's children must come to adopt. When there is more than enough for everyone, no society can so arrange its economy that the larger segment of its population, including tens of millions of defenseless children, are precluded from full access to all its know-how and resources so that life itself is threatened, and then call itself either democratic or civilized. Such arrangement is not only unjust and dishonest. It reeks of sheer barbarism.

But the right to life has to be extended to those beyond our own borders, whatever their skin-color, whatever their momentary ideological persuasion, whatever their country. They are feeling, struggling, aspiring human beings very much like ourselves. They harbor no natural hate for other human beings. What demonic tragedy that people as people can be pitted against each other in the hell of war when the needs, the yearning and the goal of all human beings are mutual!

Every Human Being's Right to Expend Effort

Although all inalienable rights are interrelated, each bolstering and expanding all others, the "right to work" is most important in the eyes of the average person because of its practical implications. No person finds it difficult to realize that a job means a pay check; a pay check means his ability to purchase the products and services he and his family need and desire. On the other hand, failure to procure employment means want and insecurity.

What he doesn't grasp is that the opportunity to expend effort to insure and enhance his own survival and well-being, as well as that of his loved ones, is an inherent right. It is a right he is born with. It is not a right that can be denied by government, by any institution, or by any economic structure.

What then can be the limitation on the inherent right to work? Perhaps this can be understood if we momentarily entertain a hypothetical situation. Let us suppose, for purposes of illustration, that you and your family awaken one morning to find yourselves the sole inhabitants of a small, isolated island. No other human beings occupy your new homeland. Looking around, you see that nature has bountifully supplied your island with resources. There are straight and sturdy trees out of which a home can be built. Animals and fowl abound to supply food and garments. You note the soil is lush with fertility.

Having been conditioned in a society where it was "good business" to erect fences around natural resources, you are reluctant just to help yourself to the raw stock so amply in evidence. You even make a survey of the island to assure yourself that there is not somewhere tacked to a tree a sign saying, "Keep Off—Private Property!" Finally it dawns on you that all such "property" belongs to a Beneficent Creator, and is not the result of human effort. This is the raw stock of Nature. These are the crude ingredients out of which usable products can be refined. Only the refining is required of you, and such refining is the true meaning of work.

At this point you recognize that only limitation on the standard of living you and your family can enjoy on your isolated island is your unwillingness to put forth human effort. You get the full impact of your God-given right to expend human effort in direct ratio to your willingness to fashion natural resources into finished products. There are no man-made restraints to hamper you. There are no bureaucratic quotas, or unearned dollars to devaluate you effort, or despotic monopolies to drive you out of business. You are free to exercise you full physical potential in realizing full enjoyment of the fruits of your labor.

Projecting your thinking into the future, you envision the perfecting of better tools, the increase in your scientific knowledge through experience as to better ways of growing, of harvesting and of building, and the division of labor possible with an increasing work force. You extrapolate how your island-society will progressively double, triple and multiply manifold its ability to grow food and fibres, to extract resources from land and water, and to refine all raw stock into usable products. You even foresee a future day when all manual burdens will be lifted from man's back and it will be possible for all you people to play, to learn, and to enjoy life to the fullest. In your mind's eye you behold the panorama of a virtual Paradise molded and shaped by the hand and mind of man . . .

Is this wild and exotic dreaming on your part? Are you having delusions of impractical conjecture? Or of grandeur? Nothing of the kind. You have premised your projected thinking on the two most important tenets that should underlie all economic thinking. You have constructively presupposed that all natural resources are here by the endowment of a Divine Creator and you have basically recognized every human being's right to expend unlimited effort in fashioning those resources into finished products. Not for once did it enter your thinking that institutions and "systems" could arise in your midst to circumscribe both.

How could it come about that your island community could have lesser enjoyment of the fruits of your labor just because less human effort would be required? How could it come about that the greater ability to produce could mean less and less claim against the abundance produced? How could it come about that not only machines would stand idle, but that millions of labor force would also be jobless? How could an entire nation become beggared, insecure and hopelessly indebted in a land of superabundance?

There are the questions that must and will be answered for you. Right now we want to leave you on your isolated island with the bedrock conviction that every human being possesses a God-given right to work in direct ratio to his willingness to expend effort for the better life for himself and his family. There can be no prohibitions or restraints of this exercise except a lack of raw stock. Considering the untapped oceans and our new skills in producing all kinds of synthetics, such lack is now non-existent.

The right to expend effort—either as an individual or collectively as a society—is an inherent right to partner up with Nature herself to take care of man's varied and multiple needs. No institutions or systems have a proper role in disrupting such partnership.

Their only natural and purposeful role is to implement and enhance this working compact.

Every Human Being's Right to Participate

This right is considerably more encompassing than the right of every person to expend effort. While it includes the foregoing right, it goes much further. The basic right to work does not necessarily concern itself with other persons, as we presented in the case of our island enterprise in its simplest family beginning. The right to participate immediately implies a number of person contending for expression whether their numbers are confined to a community or make up a whole nation.

The moment two or more persons assemble together, either through selection or circumstance, the right to participate interjects itself. Not only must each person have equal voice in shaping and deciding all rules but no one can be excluded from participating with equal opportunity. Likening it to our national game of baseball, no one man, or group of men, can appoint themselves as unelected umpires and arbitrarily rule that one person shall have "four strikes," another but "one strike," and still others shall be called out before they can even arise from the bench. This is tyranny and embodies none of the ingredients of a free society.

No society can be free when the individual's movements, his scope of living and his thinking are circumscribed by others to whom he gave no consent for such action. This includes all areas of human relationships whether it be social, economic or political. Every person has an inherent right to have a positive and meaningful voice in all decisions that pertain not only to the making of laws and operation of government but even more importantly, to all economic arrangements affecting his right to work and share in his nation's productive capacity. Man cannot be precluded from correcting those abuses.

The right to participate implies even more than decision-making and exercise of one's innate talents. It implies the right of having equal educational background. Under the heading, "Every human being's right to life," we stressed the individual child's right to equal sustenance, irrespective of parental ability. In the same vein, it must be contended that the individual child's right to education, until he assumes his role in adult society, transcends geographical lines, race origin, and the financial status of his parents. Every solitary child is a human being whose inherent right to participate is equal to that of any other child. He cannot be disadvantaged simply because he is defenseless in protesting his misfortune.

Lest anyone erroneously conclude that any of the foregoing even vaguely suggests children being wrested from their parents, or the setting up of a national bureaucratic kindergarten, let us dispel any such horrible notion pronto. We are compelled, by sheer necessity of presentation, to deal with the rights of human beings in the context of the current society and at the same time highlight their deeper, and more basic, significance in a constructively organized society. The perspective to be entertained is that the rights of children cannot be protected and preserved in any society where the rights of parents are flagrantly violated. The family unit is the most valid association within human relationships and the ultimate in social, economic and political environment is one in which the love and camaraderie of parent to child have top priority. Insure the full human rights of children will follow naturally and positively.

Fundamental in everyone's thinking must be the solid premise that every human being, however humble thwarted, has a potential capacity for self-improvement. Such capacity is the essence of the "breath of life" that is intrinsic in every person. It thus becomes the responsibility of society to awaken, nurture, instruct and inspire each person so all natural attributes, however dormant, might find fullest expression.

When all of mankind recognizes and has faith in the inherent good of man—at least in his capacity for good—the most powerful motivation in the universe can exert itself. This is the love motivation. It is the force that spontaneously moves every individual to help others as well as himself. It is the force that impels one to want to educate his brother rather than condemn him.

How can stigma be attached to any person when society itself has failed to assist him in putting his best foot forward? How can any person be condemned if there is understanding of the causes of his momentary misconduct or inadequacy of responsibility? How can penalty or ostracism help the person who needs the most help care by his fellowmen?

The cornerstone of a rational society must be that every person is of equal importance and every person is susceptible to improvement. But it is not only the improvement of the individual that is the end result. The over-all health and safety of the whole society is improved. Out of the over-all optimum functioning of the society arises the optimum functioning of the society arises the optimum performance of each and every individual.

The right to participate is predicated on the right of each to improve himself with the same opportunity as all others. How can each person learn self-reliance, develop character, and grow intellectually and culturally if he is denied, or restricted, in being a participant in the Game of Life?

Every Human Being's Right to Peace

Without this right, all other rights are meaningless. Man's right to negotiate differences, contend positions, and compete with others within a framework of peace supersedes all other considerations. What opportunity exists to exercise any rights if life itself is destroyed?

The history of man is stained in blood with the senseless killing of the innocent. Despite the superficial justification of war in some instances, from the standpoint of a man in battle, or his loved ones at home, all wars are a display of the irrationality of man. Murder is no less murder because it is done in uniform or because it involves great numbers. Destruction of life has been merely compounded. Man's inherent right to life has been violated en masse.

Within each human being is an inner motivation to settle his difference with his fellowman. Either from instinct or from caution, he refrains from bashing in the head of another person. Within any rational environment, he has a profound respect for life. It is external influence, always beyond his comprehension or control, which engenders in him the need to kill in order to fulfill "patriotic" and "citizenship" responsibilities. He is unaware that he is the pawn of minority forces protecting unearned wealth or seeking consolidation of political domination. Wars are never a confrontation of a people of one nation against the people of another nation.

Wars are bloody and senseless contests between economic and political power structures that employ mob psychology and mass murder as a means to an end.

To those who would cite the war between the America colonists and England as an example of a just war, it should be pointed out that this was a rebellion by the people themselves against despotic authority which had extended its oppression across the ocean to these shores. We must not confuse the right of revolution with manipulated and created wars by which the financial elite and privileged in powerful nations maneuver economic and political advantage. Revolution is something quite different. This is the constant right of any people to overthrow by force any rulership that has so usurped the rights of the people that open revolt is the only recourse left to gain their liberation.

We might further differentiate between War and Revolution by noting that wars are premised on the sacrifice of many lives that a few might profit, whereas revolutions, when their cause is just, are premised on the sacrifice of a few lives that "life, liberty and the pursuit of happiness" may be the lot of many people. Wars are dependent on conscription and involuntary servitude to execute their promotion, while revolutions are spearheaded by those who are voluntarily willing to die that the majority may live. There is a vast difference.

Wars are the product of a dangerous and irrational environment. They entail not only needless loss of life but all the waste of human effort allocated for billions of dollars in military material. What can't be humanly measured are the emotional horrors of war and its aftermath. Statistics cannot convey the anguished moans of the mortally wounded, futilely stumbling for cover. They cannot record the blood-curdling gasps of the dying soldier desperately trying to forestall death, or the vacant gaze of the mental cases or the homeless. They can't register the emptiness and tumult of both heart and spirit that are the personal Calvaries of families torn asunder. Not statistics, not even the eloquence of poetry, can portray the sorrow, the heartbreak, of loved ones to whom a husband, a son or a brother will never return. These are the intangibles of war that have scarred the hearts and souls of so many tens of millions.

And what of civilians, especially defenseless children, and their right to life, and to live in peace? It behooves us to ask some serious questions pertaining to our own lives. Who had the right to decree the fate of the women and children at Nagasaki and at Hiroshima when in two blinding flashes 200,000 human beings were burned to ashes, with those on the outskirts writhing in agony and dying from death-dealing radiation? Who had the right to decree the fate of the five million civilians in Korea, and the hundreds of thousands of bewildered civilians dying from napalm and saturation bombing in Vietnam as these pages are written?

And what of the right, even in peacetime, to explode hydrogen bombs, polluting the air with radioactive fallout, and foredooming unborn generations to stillbirth or to live in malformed bodies? Is there any indictment too strong of such bestial irreverence for life on its most innocent level?

Innocent civilians are now the real victims of modern warfare. War is no longer confined to the military. It should be a sobering thought to realize that since the turn of this century over 43,000,000 human beings have been killed! More jolting should be the realization that both Russia and the United States have a nuclear striking force that can exterminate such a mass of humanity in one horrifying onslaught, lasting only seconds. Does any mortal power, whether it be man, or institutions, or government, have the right to perpetuate such savagery on human beings?

The insanity of man in waging war has now reached dimensions of destructive power that if unleashed would destroy all life. It threatens complete annihilation of all human beings on this planet. Nuclear weaponry neither allows, nor permits, any sane alternative to peace. It poses the life-or-death question of whether mankind wants to make a real attempt toward living together or whether it wants to pursue its current path toward extinction and oblivion. The choice must be made. It cannot be postponed.

Embedded in our minds, and in our consciousnesses, must be man's inherent right to live in a world free from all killing. No mortal power has the right to extinguish the life of one solitary human being to settle differences between men or between nations. The first law of nature is the preservation of life, not its destruction.

The right to life itself is inherent and irrevocable. No man, no group, no nation or set of nations, can play God and destroy a human being. Whereas it is readily conceded that no one person can have the power to annihilate all of mankind, it must be equally accepted that neither can all of mankind have the power to destroy one solitary person. The principle underlying both is the same.

Voluntary sacrifice of one's life that another's might be saved is another matter. This is man's noblest act in behalf of a fellow human being. It underscores man's own recognition of the sacredness of life.

Chapter 5

MAN'S INFINITE SEARCH FOR INDENTITY

I T MAY COME as a surprise to many readers that the right to religious freedom is not set down as a specific inherent right by itself. Although it is indisputable that any person's right to his own worship and his own beliefs should be inviolate, in its most basic context, religion cannot be separated from any aspect of human relationships. The same is true in trying to separate man from his infinite environment. From the touch of a baby's hand to the undefined periphery of space, man is part of all that surrounds him.

Broadly speaking, religion encompasses man's endless search to establish relationships with an Infinite Universe, understanding his relationship with all that has been created, and so ultimately identifying himself in the whole scheme of existence. Viewed in this context we are dealing with all man's coded knowledge in all fields of science, all man's coded knowledge in all fields of science, we are dealing with all the postulates of human rights, and we are dealing with all the postulates of human rights, and we are dealing with his place in a literal society of rules, institutions and government. To fulfill this encompassment there can be no limitation on the scope of religion.

We have already alluded to the intriguing revelation of modern science that man falls midway between the smallest particle in the nucleus of the atom and the farthest outreaches of space. Looking inward and outward man is at the very hub of his existence. It is at this central position that he as observer is involved in the whole life process of trying to understand all that surrounds himself and to find personal identity.

In its broadest sense it might be said that the foregoing framework encompasses all philosophy, all knowledge, all manifestations of life and matter. It is man in relative conjunction with all these that gives rise to the formulation of his religious convictions and projections.

Religion, as we would define it, is man's relentless endeavor, through increased understanding, to display rational behavior in a rational cosmic environment. It is man's infinite quest to belong and to live in harmonious and compassionate relationship with all life in a role of full participation.

Confining religion simply to crystallized and dogmatic beliefs, or to traditional rituals of worship, is to limit tragically its fuller potentialities.

Yet such area of convictions must be inviolately reserved to each person. What a man wants to conjecture as to his spiritual origin, or as to his existence after death, is strictly within the province of the individual. Such belief has no bearing on anyone else. It is solely a matter of personal persuasion. Nor should any person be restricted in any way in converting others to his particular religious beliefs.

The orthodox Christian who believes in an ultimate Judgment Day, when the good and the bad shall be judged for their conduct, cannot be denied his right to so believe. The Hindu has the right to believe in Nirvana and his ultimate reunion with Brahma. The same right belongs to Buddhists, reincarnationalists of the west, spiritualists, agnostics, atheists or whatever you please. These beliefs have no direct bearing on literal human relationships, although there is valid argument that they often reflect personal dispositions respecting the moral and ethical makeup of society.

It is the conviction of this writer that religious institutions, as institutions, have drifted far astray from the pristine precepts of their original founders. In candid appraisal, they have clothed themselves with superficial ritual, and enshrouded themselves with an air of sanctimony that completely beclouds any understanding of how man should treat man in a Good Universe. Lost are the basic teachings of the inspired leaders who appeared in mortal flesh to point a way that the spiritual essence of man might find expression.

Across the breadth of our land, over 300,000 churches and religious edifices dot the landscape and line city thoroughfares. They lay claim to a total membership of over 125,000,000 Americans who replenish church treasuries to the extent of several billion dollars per annum. Each Sunday morning, supposedly learned men of God mount their pulpits and purport to instruct their congregations on how to walk in the footsteps of the Man who stands at the pinnacle of their religion.

What a hollow mockery they have made of His dynamic teaching!

It would be unfair to indict all men of the cloth for the passive role of the vast network of churches throughout the land. Despite the censures of institutional superiors or domineering lay boards, there are spiritual leaders who assail existing injustice, and plead for social reform that God-given reights might be exercised. They see the sheer hypocrisy in professing the brotherhood of man and then not practicing it.

It is also unfair to indict the larger part of the membership of church organizations. They are simply a cross-section of America seeking to fulfill their religious inclinations. That they don't demand more spiritual satisfaction for their hard-earned dollars, and thus literally sustain their own dearth of spirituality, is another matter. At the same time it must be taken into account that the more affluent, and the most privileged, in our society are the principal pillars supporting all major church organizations. Such members are the least disposed toward altering the status quo and thus improving man's circumstance as a whole.

Outside of furnishing more wholesome recreational facilities for the youngsters in our society, and seasonal and spasmodic gestures of charity, there is little that can be said for institutional religion in America. To date, it has crystallized into more of a hindrance to man's spiritual progress than serving to inspire man to cooperative brotherhood that individual excellence might be achieved.

No church can lay rightful claim to believing in the ministry of Man of Nazareth and not stand firmly in the fore front challenging the injustices, the evils, the exploitation that afflict the nation. The churches should be the first to denounce the Pharisees and Hypocrites that have turned the nation into a den of thieves. But that would be sedition indeed to the abnormal powers that dominate, and few are the modern "Christians" who are willing to be crucified for principle.

It is much easier to keep in the good graces of the usurers, the advertisers, the demagogues, the plutocrats in our midst, than to show genuine compassion for the millions hungry, cold and helpless. It is more comfortable to assemble in million-dollar edifices and parrot beseechment to God than to walk in the vanguard of the destitute, jobless and sick who have no tithing to pay for pipe organs or ornate masonry piled awkwardly skyward. It is much simpler to ask troubled humanity to have a "change of heart" than to be "about the Father's business" creating an environment within which the goodness in man will automatically display itself.

The self-righteous applaud loudly, and defend piously, the "Christian ethic" and persistently plead the right to invoke the "word of God" in all assemblies, especially in those of their children. Yet all the sanctimony, all the sacrificial tithings, and all the Gideon Bibles piled mountain-high, cannot alter the honest appraisal that the preachments of the Man of Galilee have be relegated to the status of something to be professed but little practiced. If the man Jesus were to make an unannounced appearance, few would recognize Him, let alone accept Him. Institutionalized Christianity would be in the forefront clamoring and shouting, "Crucify Him! Crucify Him!"

There is no attempt here to be unduly harsh indicting institutionalized Christianity. It has been singled out from other major religions only because it is the predominant persuasion in our own nation. Our reproach is based on the fact that "churchianity" in this country is a multi-billion-dollar enterprise that affords little guidance or inspiration to its tens of millions of adherents for a realistic betterment of society. Whereas it has the organizational and membership strength effectively to challenge injustice and inequity, it passively defends a national circumstance wherein man is increasingly degraded instead of uplifted. Assuredly, its sins of omission far outweigh its sins of commission. The seriousness of its dereliction, however, lies in its failure to champion human relationships based on the precepts of the Teacher to whom it purports to give full allegiance.

There are valid historical questions raised as to the fullness and accuracy of the preachments of Jesus as presented to us through the main Biblical translations. It must also be noted that his ministry is preserved and made of record only through the writings of those who followed, and that He Himself set down no personal attestments. This circumstance, however, need not lessen the import of the message that is attributed to Him or the acceptable reality of His mission.

Our unshakeable belief in Man of Nazareth lies in the fact that He by word and deed epitomizes man's potential for both altruism and personal achievement. Consistently, he emphasized the importance of the least among men, subordinated all material things to the spiritual enhancement of man, and implored man to treat his neighbor the way he in turn wished to be treated. There was neither pretense nor sham in His person or conduct. Nor was He a stickler over the foibles and fallibilities of faltering humanity.

His message was directed to all peoples. However, He devoted the larger part of His time to the downtrodden, those burdened with "sin" and illness, and those who had lost faith in themselves and in life itself. To them He reached out a compassionate hand, restoring their bodies and rekindling in them a belief in the goodness and purpose of life and an acceptance of their individual potential for performance. He left no room for distrust and hate and espoused the brotherhood of man through a compact of universal respect for each other. This is the dynamic import of His teaching.

How far a supposedly Christian nation has wandered from the vigorous and forceful teachings of the Man who walked the shores of Galilee nearly two thousands year ago! Can you envision Him seeking out the most privileged in our midst, sipping cocktails with the money-changers, the plutocrat of monopoly, the strategizing politicians, and extolling the virtues of a social structure of "everyone for himself and let the devil take the hindmost"?

Or would it seem more likely that He would be found walking the hard and joyless sidewalks of our rat-infested slum areas, traversing the barren and desecrated hills of the Appalachias of our nation, and taking counsel with the millions jobless, the millions unable to pay for proper medical care, the millions turning to crime in ignorance, frustration or desperation, and the millions mentally breaking from the stresses of an irrational society?

Can you envision the Man of Galilee turning a deaf ear to the cries of little children whose bodies are malformed from lack of nourishment? Or being oblivious to the anguish and heartache and emptiness that afflict so many bewildered fathers and mothers? Or do you think He would, cowardly, seek escape from all such degradation of body and spirit, by finding sanctuary in an ornate cathedral far removed where He might simply intone platitudes of piety relating to some distant time of saintly bliss?

The Man of Peace was an actionist, a doer of good deeds, an advocate of social reform that all human beings might enjoy the good life. He was no namby-pamby sentimentalist, who spoke in hushed tones lest He be overheard mentioning evil. He kowtowed to no one, but formed a scourge of cords and drove the money-changers from the temple. To the economic and political power-blocs of His day, He was a seditionist, and they persecuted Him and slew Him for His "tipping over of existing institutions."

Belatedly, there is need for a revitalizing of the true message of the Founder of Christianity. No longer can those who profess to His leadership simply meet on Sunday morning, closet themselves in an atmosphere of solemnity, sing praises to the "Glory of God," and then for the rest of the week show no realistic concern for groping, suffering, and unanchored human beings. Such allegiance is shameful pretense and utterly without meaning.

What of Jesus' admonition, "If any man serve me, let him follow me!"?

To understand the real ministry of Jesus is to believe in the dynamism of the precepts He enunciated. But it is more than belief. It is to embrace them so that their beauty and strength constantly shape's one's outlook and one's conduct. To accept His teachings is to recognize that He encompassed all of creation in its relationship even to the lowliest amongst men, that each could find the "kingdom within" as he gained increasing harmony with the laws and functioning of an infinite Universe. "All that I do, ye shall do, and even greater things than I do, ye shall do," expressed the latent capability He saw in every individual.

In the whole field of human relationships, He pleaded the simple rule of "treating others the way you wish to be treated." If you had done wrong, acknowledge your error—and then be about the pursuit of good deeds that you might amend your ways of misconduct. A people thus displaying genuine compassion for each other could build a literal society which would exemplify "They will be done, **on earth** as it is in Heaven." This is the promise of Christianity. It awaits fulfillment.

The individual's "right to freedom of religion" embodies all other rights. There can be no limitation to its scope of application. It is all of life and as such it excludes no field of knowledge or framework of human endeavor. It encompasses the goal of every man to understand himself and all that surrounds him. It is the science of knowing and the art of living.

It is man's infinite search to identify himself and find harmony with all life and all of creation. In this context, religion is the supreme prerogative of every individual.

Chapter 6

A QUICK GLIMPSE INTO THE PAST

T HE REASON why so many people are confused about their rights, about how society should be arranged, and what the basic concepts are that should underlie all social order is because they stubbornly refuse to let go of erroneous or outdated concepts of the past. Such refusal stems either from ignorance or from the fact that conditioning of mind precludes them from questioning that which is traditional and that which time has enshrouded with a cloak of authority. In consequence, they are neither emotionally nor intellectually equipped to let go of the old, however unworkable.

Many storehouses could be filled with volumes covering the economic and political histories of all of the countries of the world. One could prospect away back to the time of the caveman when only the crudest tools existed by which to provide for gurgling broods and trace through all the emerging civilizations from which most of our forebears came. But this would little serve our purpose, even if we set down the merest skeleton outline.

For our purposes, it is sufficient to start with that period of European history known as the Age of Feudalism which marked the latter part of the Middle Ages and is generally identified in time as ending with the 18th Century. We are particularly interested in focusing our attention on that period since it covers those years during which America was discovered and colonized. The economic and political conditions which then existed in Europe, from which our forebears escaped, left no small impact on their thinking. Some of their concepts of economics were to persist not only through the building of this nation, but are with us yet today.

There is no need to go into a lot of historical detail pertaining to the Middle Ages and the Age of Feudalism. The chronological ascensions to power of the despots, the emperors, and the repetitious royalties with Roman numerals attached are boring unless one is a student of history. The same goes for the continuous wars and intermittent civil strife that stains all the pages of European historical sequences. At the same time it would be a distorted picture to think of that whole period as consisting only of despots and wars.

Out of this era came the real beginning of science, advanced shipbuilding, and moveable type, as well as major contributions to art and literature. But this phase of that period is not what concerns us. Our concern is to grasp simply the basic relationship of the people to their means of eking out an existence. It is here that we come to appreciate the earliest premises for our economic and political relationships.

Landlord and Serf

Shorn of all trappings, European history up to, and including, the Age of Feudalism can be reduced to the broad picture of a whole span of time, covering a thousand years, in which the overwhelming majority of mankind slaved, and fought, and died for the power-blocs which owned the land and dominated politically. This is not to say that there weren't circumstances in which land barons treated their serfs with some degree of humanness. It is to say that the rank and file were dependent for their livelihood exclusively on parceled out plots of land, under such an arrangement of servitude that the landlords were absolute masters over the people.

Although the Age of Feudalism assumed varied forms of contractual agreements, depending upon whether the dominating forces were despotic kings, powerful nobility, or the overweening influence of the church, the end result was the same. A small group, who owed their position either to birth or force of arms, owned and controlled the land, and the great mass of humanity tilled the land for a pittance of what they produced. Productive capacity was limited to a strong back, a good pair of hand and the whim of the landlord.

When we are considering this distant time, and the crude implements for producing human necessities, it is quite easy to recognize the elementary circumstance that existed. If an individual and his family did not have shelter and food to sustain life. Access to land meant survival. It was as simple as that. It is likewise to appreciate that when the individual and his family were directly dependent on the land for their sustenance, they in turn were directly the political captives of those who owned the land and determined its availability for use.

Right here we can set down an inescapable axiom that bears on all degrees of economic and political freedom. It hold as true today in our own complex society as it did during the elementary society of the Age of Feudalism. It is the broad context within which all natural rights of individuals are permitted to function. Mark this well:

The extent of any people's political freedom is in direct ratio to their economic freedom. They are inseparable.

Now it is quite evident that when the vassal, under feudalism, got down on his knees and placed his hands between those of his lord, swearing absolute obedience to his dictates, his was a condition of abject political servitude. We in this modern day of "elections" and political "parties" readily condemn such denial of individual liberty. What hasn't dawned on our thinking yet is the realization that while productive capacity is now something quite different from the mere crude cultivation of land, the people's present lack of true sovereignty is directly related to their economic dependence on the few who own and direct the nation's productive potential. The only difference is that our condition of servitude is couched in more technical language and is more devious of execution. The "despotism" is not so obvious and the "tyranny" is not so direct.

It is a long road from the feudalism of Europe to the more sophisticated feudalism of the Twentieth Century. Two specific contrasts will become patent when we understand the analogous situation that exists today. The vassal knew that he was a vassal. Today the average American is unaware. Secondly, it was in the interest of the landlord to be directly concerned in maintaining the well-being of his serfs because he lived directly off their labor. Today no such personal relationship exists. Under current "capitalism", equally feudalistic in principle, man is dispensable and the monopolists of industry and finance assume no moral obligation for the well-being of human beings. All human considerations are secondary to profits and power.

Imperialistic Onslaught

The age-old conflict over who should control the tools of production has plagued mankind since the beginning of time. We have purposely started with a quick glance at European feudalism because here we observe the most obvious conditions under which human beings are controlled and subjugated. In the despotism of kings, nobility and clergy, we observe man's every move and expression dictated by direct tyrannical domination. There was no middle road. There was no camouflage hiding the line between ruler and the ruled.

It should therefore be apparent that when our forebears first arrived on American soil, well implanted in their minds was the importance of land as the prime means of providing for their needs. However, it must be noted that the colonization of the New World was not prompted by an avalanche of the oppressed and mistreated seeking freedom on distant shores. Of course these came, but they were only incidental to the imperialistic onslaught on the newly discovered hemisphere.

The whole era of exploration, blending into the Age of Mercantilism, was motivated by designs for wealth and power by the kings and land barons who dominated all of western

Europe. The royalties in power, despotically ruling their own subjects, were not in the business of underwriting freedom excursions to the Americas. It is well to bear in mind that feudalism was not abolished in England until 1662 and it did not end in France until the French Revolution in 1789.

Whereas the Spaniards resorted to most brutal murder and intrigue in conquering Mexico and all of South America except Brazil, the English, the French and the Dutch were able to employ less terroristic tactics in occupying the eastern coast of North America. All colonization nevertheless had the same underlying drive. The crowned heads and the commercial enterprises of Europe were desperate in their lust for virgin wealth and the expansion of their empires. It was an international treasure hunt, and exported to the New World the feudalistic principle that had enslaved all of Europe for a thousand years.

Anyone who has read the colonial history of this nation knows that the whole era was one of granting charters or proprietary rights to those who held positions of favoritism with royalty. Trading companies, commercial interests, and the privileged, landed and clerical, were the grantees of both of the foregoing instruments of colonization. Not only did such favored interests engage in all exploitive tactics in the parceling out of their grants of land but they brought along indentured workers to perform enforced labor. It was at this stage of American history that the scourge of imported slavery began. Nearly half a million Negroes were transported in chains to be auctioned off like cattle. Despite the elimination of the auction block, and passage of legal restraints against involuntary servitude, this degradation of human beings was still to be in evidence over two hundred years later.

Two Rebellions

As it had been true in Europe, it was expected that control of the source of production would mean control of the people who were dependent on the land for their livelihood. However, colonial conditions were quite different from those then obtaining in Europe. The best laid plans were to be foiled and to go awry. To begin with, there was more land than could be controlled. As the farmers were abused or became indebted to their landlords, they moved farther west, availed themselves of new land, and carved out new existences. They weren't imprisoned, with no place to escape to, as they had been on the fiefs in feudalistic Europe.

Also with increased immigration to America, the numbers vastly increased of those who had experienced the serfdom of Europe. In a new land, they envisaged practical liberation. They were susceptible to constructive leadership and the opportunity for individual expression. They were ripe for revolution.

To appreciate fundamentally the circumstance that led to the Declaration of Independence, and the subsequent adoption of the Constitution, is to recognize that there were two rebellions. One was the over-all rebellion against the perpetual, intolerable abuses of the English Crown. The other was an inner rebellion against the landed aristocracy, the shrew commercial interests, and the debt-merchants who wielded abnormal influence within the colonies. It is vitally important to take cognizance of this backdrop in trying to understand what ensued in the actual writing of the Constitution.

There is no more dramatic and inspiring chapter in the history of the nation than the fight for independence and the ultimate founding of our constitutional republic. Out of the throes of compounding abuse and the interminable injustices meted out to the colonists by England arose an irrepressible dynamism of American leadership that could not be subdued. It beheld not only the necessity but the ideal opportunity for establishing a new nation based on the governmental concept that the people themselves should exert supreme rulership.

It is not the glories of the American Revolution that will now engage our attention. Every schoolchild is familiar with "the shot heard 'round the world" and the final surrender of

Cornwallis at Yorktown. We are concerned with the actual adoption of a written constitution that founded our nation and set it on the road to work out its own destiny. Under its guidance must come the fortunes or misfortunes of the nation in denouement both of time and event.

We are unwilling to accept that the founders of this nation were all incarnated saints, that they were imbued with singular purpose of establishing liberty and justice and that they adopted an infallible Constitution. Such blind ideology may connote a deep reverence for one's country but it is tragically misleading. Nor do we accept that to point out failures or omissions in the Constitution in any way belittles the enormous stride that was made in the social evolution of mankind.

Chapter 7

A NEW NATION EMERGES

T HE CONSTITUTION of the United States was the first written social contract premised on self-government. It was designed and adopted, by men who believed, theoretically at least, in the right of the people themselves to govern themselves. Considering the pressures of the times, the serious divergence of viewpoints, and the influence of predatory groups, it is incredible that the final instrument embodied as much as it did in the way of human rights. While we do not want to diminish by one iota the importance of the achievement, we do not want to let sentimental idealism preclude an unprejudiced appraisal.

We purposely presented, although very sketchily, the feudalistic conditions of Europe and the colonial struggle leading up to the fight for independence. Our specific reason for doing so was to underscore the obvious circumstance that economic freedom was in direct ratio to political freedom. Put conversely, those who dominate politically are those who own or control the tools or means of production.

No one should have any difficulty in recognizing that the serf, under European feudalism, was directly beholden to the dictates and whims of his landlord. It is painfully apparent that his will was completely subordinated to the will of the owner of the piece of land from which he had directly to obtain his food. In the case of the Negro slaves who were brought to America and placed in human bondage, and, to a lesser degree, the indentured workers who contracted for their passage to these shores, we also have no difficulty in appreciating their state of serfdom.

When we take note of the corporate charters and proprietary land grants under which the privileged were the monied emissaries of the tyrannical government of George III, we also can recognize that the abuses heaped on the colonists were directly due to the fact that without economic freedom there could be no political freedom.

Why Not Economic Safeguards?

However, when we come to consider the time after the colonies had successfully won their political independence, and had full opportunity to insure projected liberty for all the people, we are confronted with a manifest paradox. Why didn't the Founding Fathers make positive provision for the economic independence of each and every citizen so that maximum survival and well-being would be the natural condition of all generations to follow?

What must be borne in mind is that while an industrial revolution was taking place in Europe, altering drastically the whole complexion of man's arrangements for eking out his material livelihood, the chief preoccupation in America was the culmination of a political revolution. Upon the Jeffersons, the Washingtons, the Madisons, and all the dynamic men that history had entrusted with the founding of a new nation, fell the pressing task of writing a constitution which would give political identity to a newly won independence. Economic considerations, the lack of which would lead to serious maladjustments at a later time, were left to belated introspection. Even so, many of the framers of the Constitution voiced serious misgivings at the time respecting the failure to embody adequate economic provisions in the instrument they were writing.

It would seem evident that the Founding Fathers were primarily concerned with setting up a government, provided by a written constitution, which would be broadly responsive to the wishes and the needs of the people. They were willing to place utmost reliance on the wisdom of the people to modify or enlarge the provisions they had set down in accordance with changing conditions or unforeseen circumstances.

It is the shallow and conditioned thinking of the present day that concludes that an assemblage of saints, with godlike omniscience, fashioned a document that need not, and must not, be changed. The fact that the Founders laid no claim to such achievement, but in fact overwhelmingly expressed in their writings that "the dead shall not govern the living," seems to carry little weight with those modern "patriots" who are unwilling to fore go a night of television in order to read a minimum of history.

The important perspective that must be entertained is that the Constitution that was adopted was the best that well-intentioned men could shape during the times in which it was written. When thought is given to the then-existing turmoil, the dissensions, the controversies, and the pressures of propertied groups, and particularly to the circumstance that the whole gesture was a revolutionary experiment in self-government, we of this era in history can only marvel at the resulting product that was incubated and delivered.

The Intent of the Constitution

The Preamble to the Constitution states:

> We the people of the United States, in order to form a more perfect union, establish justice, insure domestic Tranquility, provide for the common defense, promote the general welfare, and secure the Blessing of Liberty to ourselves and to our Posterity, do ordain and establish this Constitution for the United States of America.

Here in fifty-two words were enumerated the whole intent and reason for the new government that was being established.

Here was clearly set down, although in general terms, the predetermined goal of the nation. Everything that followed in the setting up of functioning government, legislating of laws, executing of laws, interpreting of laws, the delegation of powers, and the provisions for amendment were for the sole purpose of achieving the explicit goals of the Preamble. This was the prevailing intent of the Founding Fathers.

Strange that it should be relegated nearly to obscurity when people of this day speak of our government and its purposes. One might as logically speak of erecting a school and making the building blueprint more important than the goal of educating the boys and girls who would be attending the school. Or to speak of a family trying to chart the route they would travel on a vacation before determining the destination of their trip.

There is no reason to find fault with the goals that were set down in the Preamble. They unquestionably reflect the thinking that motivated the signers of the Declaration of Independence. It is also pertinent to note that the first line in the Constitution reads "**We the people** of the United States" join in this agreement to achieve certain objectives. When we grasp the basic parts of social contracts, we then understand that constitutions are agreements amongst peoples, and none other. It is people, as individuals, who have the inherent rights which seek expression through mutual contract. It is they who give sanction and power to a constitution. Certainly, no individual would give his consent to any agreement, directly or indirectly, which would disservice him by giving him neither equal protection nor equitable participation.

People, Not States, Delegate Powers

An erroneous notion is entertained in this country that the original thirteen colonies, in setting up a centralized Federal government, delegated certain rights. The truth is that the States, as States, had no such "rights" to delegate. It was the sovereign people of the respective States who had the rights. It was the people who delegated some of them to the State government, and some to the Federal government.

In short, it was the **citizens** of all the States, taken collectively, that gave the Constitution sanction and authority. **People, not governmental structures, have powers which can be retained or delegated.**

When one understands the foregoing, one can grasp the fundamental error of States, or institutions, and political parties interjecting themselves between the people and their Constitution and destroying the very purposes for which the constitutional agreement was brought into being. No individual should lose sight of the fundamental premise that it is he, as a human being, who is both arbiter and beneficiary of constitutions. Whenever he is precluded from being a participant in either role, he has then become a victim of the very instrument that was to insure his meaningful and enhanced participation. Under such tyrannical circumvention, the democratic process has become supplanted by a form of despotism.

Politically, it is quite obvious that under the Constitution as originally written there was no provision for the nearly one-half million Negroes, who were in bondage, to have a voice in government. Equally excluded were all human beings who were of the fair sex. Under this circumstance alone, over half the entire population was arbitrarily denied suffrage. Isn't it somewhat hypocritical to lay claim that the nation was founded on the principle of "government by the consent of the governed"?

When it is noted that the wealthy property owners succeeded in getting written into the Constitution the power of the respective States to determine voting qualifications, and to determine educational opportunities, additional citizens were excluded from exercising the vote. This double-edged sword of political subterfuge was to persist in its diabolical injustice to the present day.

Whereas there may have been some justification in the pleading of the "States' Rightists" in the founding of the nation on the grounds that there was danger of an overlording Federal government, the position has no validity when considered in the framework of human rights. This should not be construed as any brief for Federal bureaucracy which we shall later see stems from an entirely different set of factors. Property holdings cannot supersede human rights. The rights of education and voting cannot be subjected to sectionalism. Their exercise has to be universal within the full jurisdiction of the Constitution.

The illegality of States, as lesser governmental structures, dictating the extent to which human rights should be exercised is belatedly being recognized. What twisted logic to contend that a child's right to education, and later his right to vote, should be at the mercy of geographical birth! The same is equally true for all other inherent human rights.

Belated Franchise

It was not until 1865, after the termination of a bloody Civil War, that the Negro was freed from slavery by the 13th Amendment. Then came the adoption of the 14th Amendment which was the first constitutional prohibition against the States, specifically preventing them from denying a citizen equal protection of "life, liberty and property." Shortly thereafter, under the 15th Amendment, the Negro technically was given the legal right to vote. At this late date, after a span of a hundred years, all three Constitutional Amendments have existed largely in name only.

It wasn't until well into the Twentieth Century that woman were given the right to vote. Prior to such time they fought in vain for political recognition. It took the nation's menfolk a century and a half to give their womenfolk, who bore their children, a voice in shaping the environment in which those children might have the chance to grow constructively. Consent of the governed, indeed! We can only speculate how different the history of the nation might have been if the genuine compassion toward children and sensitivity to injustice, so inherent in motherhood, had found expression in the nation's very beginning.

By the time women had been given the franchise, political parties had grown to multi-million-dollar machines—the defenders of the power-blocs that had gained monopolistic control over the nation's money and productive assets. Political sovereignty, expressed through the ballot box, had become a sham and a deception. Representative government had ceased to be responsive to either the needs or the wishes of the people.

Perspective of the Present

There is no practical purpose served by indicting the Founding Fathers for being derelict either wittingly or unwittingly. There is also no purpose served by indicting individuals or groups who could justly be called the real culprits of that time. They are all dead and buried, and belong to the past. Our concern is to take a sober look at that period of Revolutionary history and make an appraisal, free from emotions and personalities.

Viewed in retrospect, fully considering the circumstances that obtained at the beginning of the Nineteenth Century, it is not the failures of the Founding Fthers to write a Constitution that would be adequate up the centuries that is disturbing or up for criticism, but the narrow-mindedness of many people of the present who attribute an infallibility and permanence to what was created almost two centuries ago. Somehow, although unsupported by any reasoning or logic, it is taken for granted that a Constitution adopted during a strictly agricultural era, with only the most primitive means of production and person-to-person communication, would be just as proper and adequate at a time when technological refinements could produce all things to abundance and achieve instant communication among all citizens over the length and breadth of the nation. The whole consideration is absurd and lacking in perspective.

Economically, the Fifth Amendment to the Constitution did provide that life, liberty and property could not be taken from the individual without due process of law. However, there were no limitations or safeguards respecting the accumulation of property or unearned profit-taking, and here is where the chief economic defect is found and still exists.

Politically, the First Amendment was the only basic provision for insuring the sovereignty of the people

There is little question but the Founders felt that if the people had an unqualified right to freedom of speech, freedom of press, the right to peaceable assembly, and the right to petition for a redress of grievances, then the supreme power would rest with the people to air all ideas and make all needed. Not only could abuses be corrected but innovations could be adopted. Theoretically, this would be a free society. The lack of specific protections, however, was to prove otherwise. But were the framers of the Constitution to blame?

How could the men of that time foresee the rise to monopolistic power of minority groups, financial and industrial, so that newspapers would be shackled by their advertisers, that radio and TV would likewise be forced to cater to billion-dollar enterprises that foot the bill for entertainment, and that colleges would be restricted to teaching the beauties of the status quo because billion-dollar foundations wanted no disruption of an economic system under which their parent monopolies enjoyed immeasurable advantage? How could the Founding Fathers foresee that these same monopolies would control both major political parties and that the average citizen would have no meaningful choice of candidates who really represented the majority of the people? How could they foresee that ultimately there would exist in the land only the right to agree but not the right to disagree?

At the same time that we make allowance for the inability to foresee the future circumstances that would arise in the nation, we must also remember the fact that direct participation, politically, at that time, was a physical impossibility. This circumstance is what prompted representative government. Not only was there a general lack of education, certainly in the case of the Negro who was so shortly removed from extremely primitive existence, but the sheer physical difficulties of travel and communication made the principle of the "town meeting" participation in national government impossible.

However, this is no reason that checks on elected officials were not provided for by the Constitution to insure the maximum control of representatives. Even at that date the sovereign power to recall any elected candidate who ceased to act in the interests of the people and the nation.

There are ample writings bearing out the intention of those who wrote the Constitution that politically the people should be dominant. This was underscored by Thomas Jefferson when he stated:

> I know of no safe depository of the ultimate powers of society but the people themselves, and if we think them not enlightened enough to exercise their control with a wholesome discretion, the remedy is not to take it from them but to inform their discretion by education.

To those who questioned the competency of the people to rule, Jefferson retorted that if the people were competent to elect the wisest to make decisions for them, then they at the same time possessed the wisdom to make their own decisions.

The Jeffersons, the Washingtons, the Madisons, the Jays, the Thomas Paines, all who played important roles in the founding of the nation recognized that the Constitution derived all sanction and power from the people it was to serve. Politically, these men sought to achieve this end, leaving modifications up to oncoming generations. Their failure would lie in their not taking sufficient cognizance of the economic and financial forces already then at work to subvert and emasculate that which their hands and minds had brought to fruition.

The real failure lay with the people who came after who permitted themselves to become economic slaves by not recognizing that they had as much right to economic sovereignty as they had to political sovereignty. There can be no such thing as political freedom without economic freedom.

Chapter 8

LET THE DEVIL TAKE THE HINDMOST

A S WE look back at the end of the 18th Century from the vantage point of the present, we are compelled to take note of three previous circumstances that existed which bear on the failure to provide for economic sovereignty in the Constitution. Our need is only to identify them and not to overspeculate on the influence they exerted. Subsequent economic developments speak louder and demand more of our attention.

The most obvious circumstance is that there was unlimited virgin land and no one foresaw a lack of productive resources. Since farming was an independent, self-sustaining enterprise, what more economic security could be provided than access to an individual piece of property? Productive capacity was exclusively, aside from the plantations, an individual endeavor. The farmer cleared the land, planted his seeds and harvested his crops. That which he produced beyond his needs, he exchanged with his neighbors for goods of which they had excess. This was an exchange of value for value, through simple barter, and to all intents and purposes the nation's first citizens did have equal access to natural resources, and they could exercise the right to expend maximum effort for the wellbeing of their families.

The second circumstance was the influence of those who had already established themselves as large property holders, many of them owning plantations of thousands of acres with enforced slavery. Coupled with them were the debt-merchants who already had gained a throttlehold on the young nation's monetary needs. Neither group had any altruistic inclination to relinquish such holdings or control. Neither group wished any restrictive provisions written into the Constitution which would lessen their holdings or control, or which would prevent both from expanding. However, a third circumstance would seem to have been the most dominant and persuasive. Whereas America was largely agrarian in economic makeup, an entirely different set of forces were shaping the approach to production and distribution in Europe, particularly England. Out of feudalism, the direct relationships of worker-to-land, had emerged a whole new set of factors having to do with "division of labor" and "the market system." In 1769 James Watt invented the steam engine and the Industrial Revolution had erupted. Power external to man had been harnessed to work machines and the concept of group endeavor supplanted the individual worker.

Along with hiring and compensating workers came the need to provide the capital for starting new businesses, building new factories, and the whole financial influence "credit," "investment" and "debt" was to come into its own. This was by no means the inception of the money-lender or banker, but heretofore his role had been largely that of underwriting royalty in maintaining its political tyranny and defraying the costs of its military and colonial ventures. They were now to interject their influence into the economic affairs of the vast majority with consequences that would be increasingly, and disastrously, felt up the next two hundred years.

There is no doubt that most of the Founding Fathers, meeting at the Constitutional Convention in Philadelphia in 1787, struggling to write a document that would provide for political freedom, had read Adam Smith's "Wealth of Nations" which was published in 1776, the year of the Declaration of Independence. To what extent they accepted or rejected the whole theory of a self-regulating "free market" and the government "hands off" policy of **laissez faire** is immaterial. By their omission of any specific provisions for the constitutional protection of the economic sovereignty of the people, they wittingly, or unwittingly, accepted this theory for the economic life of the nation.

Additionally, the Protestant movement had been gradually evolving a philosophy which in effect blessed the accumulation of riches as a visible sign of diligence to one's "calling," thus favorable in the eyes of an exacting and cantankerous Deity. In the delightful business of piling up wealth (and consequent worldly power) the original religious basis faded inevitably from the scene.

Nation Left Unprotected

When viewed in retrospect, it is apparent that the stage had been set for the progressive, and systematic, sacking of the nation. Although much blood and treasure had been expended to wrest the nation from the clutches of overseas despotism, it had nevertheless been left economically vulnerable to the voracious and predatory who were already gnawing at its unseasoned foundations. Instead of the fundamental, inherent, economic rights of the individual being written into the Constitution, making them inviolate to each citizen, the material fortunes or misfortunes of the people were left dependent on the premise of "everyone for himself and the devil take the hindmost!"

Out of this "might-makes-right" philosophy came all the gimmicks of debt-money capitalism that were ultimately to lodge the major productive assets of the nation in the hands of the few, with the majority left without equity or purchasing power against that which they in the accumulate had made possible. This was the philosophy of economics that held that if all the forces in society were turned loose in the "market place" arena, with no holds barred, out of such free-for-all would come just rewards to all contestants.

It was only necessary to identify it as the "free enterprise" and the "open market" system. An unsuspecting nation was to accept such ambiguous terms as a national ideology.

Over the years, a preponderant number of Americans have accepted that "capitalism" is synonymous with our most cherished ideals, that somehow it is the handiwork of our Founding Fathers, and that in a basic sense, it embodies and gives exercise to the inherent rights of the individual. This is sheer nonsense. In reality, it is none of these. Equally nonsensical is the mental conditioning which indicts anyone who questions the workability of "capitalism" as being an adherent to some type of foreign doctrine or "ism."

Belatedly, people are recognizing that there is nothing sacred about the origin of capitalism. There was no proviso for it in the Constitution. It was, in fact, a self-developing and self-perpetuating system whose credentials to operate stemmed from the absence of any constitutional safeguards to protect the economic sovereignty of the people. It was the "free-for-all" theory that if all forces in society—workers, management and capital—were allowed to compete openly and freely to the maximum extent of their influence, the nation would enjoy the maximum material benefits.

However, American capitalism was not to come into full flower until the Industrial Revolution occurred during the middle of the Nineteenth Century. By the turn of the Twentieth Century, the whole debt-money, capitalistic economy had turned the corner and was headed down a road that could only lead to collapse. It was a matter of time. It was inevitable because it contained within itself the flaws whose effects must inescapably become more devastating and lasting.

Ironical indeed is the fact that it was to be man's flagrant misuse of his own advanced knowledge that would administer the **coup de grace** to a system of producing and distributing that made love of the dollar more important than love of man himself.

We are not interested in quibbling over whether or not our economic system is called "capitalism," "free enterprise," "the profit system," or is even enshrined with a holiness attesting to some divine infallibility. Our interest lies only in appraising its workability and its justness in providing for the economic needs of each and every human being. More accurately, we want to bring out into the light of day its built-in flaws that have resulted in the current plight of the whole nation.

When we gain a more comprehensive understanding of the workings of private capitalism, we will clearly grasp that it was inevitable that· spiraling indebtedness, confiscatory taxes, bureaucratic welfarism, and perpetual militarism would be the denouements of an economic system that thrived on imbalance between production and distribution.

Violation of both the economic and parallel political rights of all human beings would be compounded as the scientific and productive growth of the nation expanded.

However sugar-coated and camouflaged, the basic workings of private capitalism simply give license to the strong and cunning to mulct and exploit the less fortunate. They are the means by which man's most predatory instincts are gratified. They have put a premium on economic savagery.

A new nation had been born. Out of wilderness and fertile soil that stretched from ocean to ocean was to be built a new civilization. How that civilization was shaped and how it grew is now all history. Our concern is to understand how a nation so bountifully blessed with resources, and so amply sprinkled with men of wisdom, and so populated with a whole people equal to every challenge of toil and adventure, could ultimately become the hapless victim of the present. What forces would thwart the visions of those who saw in the progressive improvement of tools and knowledge the betterment of peoples? What economic arrangements would make the people politically impotent to eradicate injustice from their midst and to shape their own destiny?

Answers to these questions will consume the balance of this book. Self-evident will be the adjustments that can and must be made. The will to make them, and the decision to make them, will rest with the people.

Out of understanding is always engendered the courage to act with purpose.

Chapter 9

INHERENT FLAWS OF PRIVATE CAPITALISM

I N THE previous chapter we stated that private capitalism was a self-developing and self-perpetuating economic system whose credentials to operate stemmed from the absence of constitutional provisions to protect the inherent economic rights of the people. We repeat this definition because it gives us the necessary backdrop against which to analyze and consider the raw workings of the capitalistic system. From the beginning it has been the **absence** of any rules or limitations that has permitted the unchecked economic exploitation of the majority.

Private capitalism is an economic system that has been, and is, an open-ended organism directly dependent for its survival and growth on exploiting the work and resources of both the nation and its citizenry, on escalating unearned profits and assets, and on keeping the people politically subservient.

It is a system of production and distribution that is parasitical in nature and predatory in function.

To the average American, conditioned in all the niceties of "free enterprise" and the "sanctity" of profit and contract, the foregoing sounds like an overly harsh description. It is only when he gains a working knowledge of how private capitalism operates, with all its ramifications of unearned claims and progressive concentrations of both the nation's natural wealth and producing assets, that he recognizes the injustice and unworkability of the system.

He can then comprehend how a nation could develop technologically from an exclusively agrarian society to the most powerful industrial society in the world while at the same time there could be such flagrant abuse and disservice to the majority of its citizenry.

The prime objective of this chapter is to commence to get our first grasp as to how the system as a system operates. In follow-up chapters, we want to get further knowledge of the **modus operandi** of private capitalism so we can understand why the whole socio-economic history of the nation has been one of successive panics and depressions, of unemployment and persistent poverty, of foreclosures and financial insolvency, and why there has been a constant pattern of **unmet** needs while at the same time there has been **unused** capability.

We want to grasp as we can why the vast majority of people, the hundreds of millions who have lived in this nation, have not enjoyed progressive material security commensurate with the progressive improvement of the nation's tools and scientific know-how.

Even more to the point, we want to understand how this nation of ours, containing within its own borders all its own resources, all its own manpower, and all its own technological skill to turn raw stock into an abundance of goods and services, could degenerate to its current plight of irretrievable indebtedness, tens of millions caught in the throes of poverty and joblessness, larger and larger segments slated to be removed from the economy, and the whole society permeated with ethical breakdown and violence.

In whose interest, at whose dictation, has the nation progressively lost its ability to utilize its labor, its resources and its ingenuity for the good life for all its people?

The foregoing questions can only be answered by penetrating through the whole maze of technical economic jargon and ideological window-dressing and identify the inherent flaws of private capitalism. It has been the compounding of these flaws that has been responsible for all the economic inequities the nation has endured and still endures, and which has sounded the death knell of the system as a system.

Briefly, the fallacious premises of private capitalism could be summarized as follows:

1. Unearned "profit-taking" is both morally and ethically indefensible. This is so whether we are considering the unearned profit gained by one of our forebears in buying and selling a horse, a piece of land or his musket, or whether we are considering current despotic monopolies which deprive workers of their just wages and deprive consumers of their just purchasing power through price-fixing.

Even if it were possible to provide each person with the same advantages and privileges to wage economic warfare with the other fellow, there would be no moral justification for the act of outmaneuvering a fellow human being of that which is his and of that which he needs.

2. Private capitalism places no limitation on the accumulation of wealth in either property holdings which can be acquired or purchasing power exercised. As a result, fences are built around the nation's natural resources and producing assets, precluding their availability and utilization for the majority. At the same time the few possess claims against the produced goods and services exceeding their physical ability to consume and use them. Conversely, the majority have been denied their rightful claims against goods and services which they could consume and use.

3. Private capitalism completely negates the paramount goal of any sound and equitable socioeconomic arrangement-that production should be geared to the needs and requirements of the nation and its citizens. Instead production is geared primarily to the acquisition of assets and resources resulting in the economic subjugation of human beings.

4. Private capitalism thrives and exists on the false premise that a sovereign people are not to be trusted, through their government, with the issuance of their own money and credit which would give the nation a debt-free and interest-free money supply. Loans, liens, mortgages and all forms of indebtedness— are thereby the instruments employed by the nation's private bankers and debt merchants to bondage the whole citizenry. They are the instruments by which claims are placed against

future earnings in order that the people can buy at present that which they have already produced.

5. Private capitalism inevitably leads to despotic monopoly which by its very nature makes a farce of all the economic idealisms of "free competition," "supply and demand," the "open market" and "free enterprise."

6. Private capitalism places the whole nation at the mercy of autocratic monopolists, industrial, financial and political, who arbitrarily control not only the amount of work the nation can do but arbitrarily dictate the degree of freedom allowed to each and every citizen.

7. Private capitalism destroys the economic sovereignty of the people. As workers, consumers and taxpayers they are denied voice and are deprived of equity in the whole economic picture. Individually, they are slaves to those who control the means of production. Without economic sovereignty, they have no political sovereignty.

8. Private capitalism provides the loopholes for circumventing all laws and constitutional provisions against depriving a person of "life, liberty and property without due process of law" and denying him "equal justice under the law."

9. Private capitalism makes inherent human rights subservient to the imposed "rights" of property. Consequently artificial entities exercise more rights than natural persons.

10. Private capitalism is dependent for its final existence on burgeoning welfarism, brutal war and the police state to take care of both the unpurchasable production and dispensable manpower which are the inevitable results of a capitalistic economy.

11. Private capitalism alienates man from his true self and appeals to his beastliness instead of to his innate goodness.

In order to understand the unworkability of private capitalism, it is necessary to comprehend, at least broadly, eight distinct areas that reveal the fallacious premises underlying the private capitalist system. They are:

1. Profit and the Open Market
2. Surplus men and surplus goods.
3. Instruments for bailing out the "system."
4. Side effects of the "system."
5. Outcasts of the "system."
6. Private issuance and control of money.
7. Artificial entities versus human beings.
8. Political parties versus the sovereign people.

All the foregoing are interlocking, interrelated and interdependent in making up the system of private capitalism. Yet we can consider them separately in order to understand the part each plays in the whole system.

Chapter 10

"PROFIT" AND THE OPEN MARKET

S O INGRAINED in the average person's thinking is the right to "extract profit" that it is almost impossible to command his attention long enough to convince him of its fallacy. Aware of the fact that wages alone are not sufficient by which to become a millionaire, he sees in the **unlimited** right to siphon off unearned claims from the economy the avenue by which he too can pyramid his ownership of property and assets and be numbered among the fabulously wealthy.

Thus, those who already are the chief beneficiaries and controllers of the economic system, who fully realize that the very success of the few is directly dependent on disadvantaging the vast majority, encourage the fiction that every person has an equal opportunity to become an affluent and dominant capitalist.

It is, and has been, the blind acceptance of this deceit, more than anything else, that has furnished the glue that has held the system of private capitalism intact.

Up the generations the people have been propagandized to believe that without the inducement of "profit" no one would work, the wheels of industry would come to an abrupt halt, and only some form of regimentation would be an alternative. When we grasp that "profit"—in all cases where it represents an unearned gain beyond anything tangible added to either goods or services—is simply camouflaged **theft,** the contention that it is the only incentive to work and progress is to debase the integrity of man and to subordinate his spirituality.

It is not difficult to appreciate that during the earliest history of our nation, the fallacious gimmick of "profit" was largely confined to individual transactions, except for the manipulations of the nation's money supply which we will give specific treatment later, and such isolated transactions were absorbed into the economy without much disruptive effect. Also, our forebears, prior to the era of mechanization, lived primarily off the land and enjoyed the standard of living directly related to their own personal expenditure of effort. Ample land waited to be cleared and cultivated and simple barter equalized over-production and under-production.

What pertained to the family-farm also pertained to the small shop. Both were self-sustaining operations and both small farmer and small proprietor were arbiters of their own livelihoods.

However, even then it should have been recognized that when the farmer bought a $50 horse, neither curried him nor fed him, and immediately sold him for $100, the first party had realized an unearned profit of $50 for which he made no contribution. In short, the second buyer had been deprived, or had stolen from him, $50 in earned purchasing power. The important thing to note, however, is that in such individual transactions there had simply been an exchange of purchasing power in the profit-taking adventure. Although morally and ethically unjustified, the gain and loss had been restricted to two parties. Even to this day such shrewd bargaining, commonly identified as "Yankee trading," is engaged in and no one would contend that such individual profit-taking is responsible for any of the economic panics or disruptions that have periodically plagued the over-all economy.

Inescapable, however, is the fact that from the beginning, it has been the failure to recognize the fallacy of unearned profit in terms of the individual that has led the people to accept blindly unearned profit-taking as quite proper in commercial transactions involving an entire citizenry. What wasn't recognized is that the compounded gains of the few are the compounded losses of the majority with the accumulative result of depriving the majority not only of their rightful and proportionate **purchasing power** but denying them rightful and proportionate equity in the productive assets which their efforts made possible.

There was no recognition that the "capital" that was used for expansion of the operating business, or that was used to start successive new businesses, reflected the efforts of labor as well as management. Even when the new enterprise was started by getting loans from the private banks, thus bringing into play new capital, such loans were made as much on the work capability of the workers as they were on the management know-how of those capitalizing the business.

The broad economic picture of the United States is a constant process of capitalizing and recapitalizing businesses using the unearned claims extracted from the whole economy. Inevitably a saturation point would be reached. Not only would virgin resources be gobbled up by a few and monopoly have precluded small businesses as contenders in the market place but the evolution of technology would have made the tens of millions of the labor force unnecessary and dispensable.

Private capitalism has been, and is, an economic system which condones, encourages and allows the few to force the majority to pay a thousand and one forms of tribute to economic masters in order to participate in the nation's economy.

All forms of rent, all forms of interest and fictitious credit, all forms of under-paid wages, and all forms of overcharged prices are the primary mechanisms for the extracting of unearned claims. It has been the unchecked accumulative effect of these unearned claims that has in turn provided the magnates of industry, and particularly expanding corporations, with **unearned capital** by which to achieve ever-increasing ownership of the nation's natural resources, its producing assets and its patented technology.

Compounded assets have led to monopolistic and despotic control of the whole economy. Simultaneously has come the bondaging of the people and their government, and the political power to coerce not only privilege legislation but to thwart any interference with the exploitive and monopolistic operations of private capitalism.

Risk, Competition, Supply and Demand

Of course, the apologist for profit-taking will perfunctorily agree that profit for one person must be another's loss. But he quickly interjects the over-all concept of the self-regulating Open Market. In so doing, he smugly proceeds to acquaint us with the factors of "risk," "free competition," and "supply and demand." Using our example of the $50-horse that was sold for $100, he points out that the original speculator didn't know that he could immediately sell and he might have spent the next three years feeding and currying an unsalable animal. Or, he points out that the buyer, who we say was euchered out of his $50, didn't have to buy from the speculator and could have wended his way into the Open Market where supply and demand would have forced the seller to charge only a competitive price.

The foregoing sounds theoretically convincing. It is the theory of so-called classical economics expounded and dinned in the ears of the people from the time they take their first breath until they are laid to rest. However, it is only the smokescreen behind which to hide the false premise of private capitalism and in particular to justify the fallacies of profit-taking.

No one denies that both "risk" and "supply and demand" are equalizing influences in the economy. What is contended here is that they are only operative in those areas where the productive assets have not been concentrated in the hands of the few. So, while the small farmer, the small businessmen, and the small manufacturer **do** fight each other competitively, the inescapable result of open-ended private capitalism is the pyramiding of productive assets in every field into the hands of a minority until monopoly **destroys** all competition.

And with the destruction of all competition, all consumers are the captive buyers of the monopolies. Where does the factor of risk enter in if the buying public is forced to pay the prices that the monopolies dictate? Where, and how, do the factors of supply and demand, and competition, enter into determining the price when the control of production is the exclusive province of monopolistic entities?

Irrefutable is the observation that the ultimate in monopolistic ownership and control is the absolute power to force the nation's buyers to pay "administered prices" that include not only the exorbitant profits accruing to the monopoly, but also the underwriting of the research and enterprise¬ expansion which makes the monopoly more dominant. The real irony lies in the fact that progressively the people, including both small businesses and farms, have been forced to underwrite their own exclusion from the economy!

It is when we grasp the power and control that monopolies exert in the current times of an automated economy with all its interlocking connections with government, the military, all media of communications, our institutions of learning and private banking that we recognize the extent of minority power over the lives of the vast majority. It is in this framework that we see the billions of dollars—the hundreds of billions-involved in technical research, in government contracts, in imperialistic wars, which are extorted out of the economy by the endless price and tax tributes paid by the people.

To speak of supply and demand as an operating principle is to deal in economic nonsense. Throughout the nation there is need for millions of new housing units to replace rat-infested tenements and the shanties of the Appalachias; there is need for tens of thousands of new schools by which to provide adequate educational facilities; there is need for more hospitals to adequately take care of those sick and injured, not to mention the dire need for the sheer basic necessities of food and clothing that would make life bearable for tens of millions of the nation's citizens. What puerile reasoning to contend that supply and demand has any reality when a productive potential exists which could easily meet the needs and demands of the nation and its people!

Human Beings Secondary

The most significant observation that the people must make in analyzing private capitalism is that the primary objective of the system is the success of business and not human beings. Goods, services and the well-being of the entire citizenry are all secondary. In fact, human beings and the goods and services they are allowed to enjoy are simply the by-products of the whole economic system.

The whole thrust of private capitalism is simply the use of people to create bigger and bigger conglomerates of wealth which increasingly exclude the people from having either purchasing power 'or ownership. The system is predicated on the overriding principle of the "maximization of profit" and as such it is doomed because its success is dependent on a few winners while the majority are the losers. There is no cognizance of the premise that human beings were not meant for systems, but that systems were meant for human beings.

In order to make private capitalism acceptable, it has been necessary to sell the people on the concept that "competition" was, and is, the only approach by which the best products, the most efficient producing of those products, and the excellence of individual performance could he achieved. No greater falsehood has been promoted and perpetuated throughout the nation's economic history. Just the opposite has resulted.

It has been the whole concept of competitive free-enterprise which has given license to those most shrewd and domineering to deprive and dominate the majority. However, neither individuals nor businesses are to be condemned as such for achieving the very success which the economic system sanctions and encourages. It is the system as a system that must be indicted and condemned.

Before you conclude this book, there will be insight given on a new order in economics that must come into being. Human beings must become paramount in any just and workable economic system. To be paramount, the people must work together instead of competing for the spoils of the system. They must have the opportunity of serving others in a cooperative approach that excludes no one from the over-all capability of the nation. In making the whole group better, to that extent is each person's well-being and safety enhanced.

While the competitive, dog-eat-dog approach may make bigger stockholders, furnish bigger cars and fancier clothes, increase statistically the Gross National Product, and create positions of dominance over others, it at the same time beggars tens of millions, breaks up families, fills our asylums and prisons, and leaves a nation of people bewildered and unanchored.

The most important economic lesson to be learned is that it is possible to have maximum efficiency of production, utilizing a nation's maximum technology, and at the same time to produce citizens that excel in character and compassion, and who achieve mastery over themselves.

Chapter 11

SURPLUS MEN AND SURPLUS GOODS

I T WAS the introduction of steam and water power that gave rise to the first factories in America. The whole concept of economics became one of group endeavor and division of labor became the structural layout of every factory. The individual's effort was multiplied manifold by use of machines and coordinated production. It all culminated in what every schoolchild knows as the Industrial Revolution. If at this point in history sound principles of economics had been adhered to, and all segments of the society had sought only the maximum wellbeing of each other, America could have set out on a road to such achievement and prosperity that neither natural hardships could have affected, nor depressions afflicted, the land. Not only was there an abundance of natural resources but power had been harnessed to do work. The lot of mankind should have become progressively easier. From the middle of the 19th Century up to the turn of the current century, the whole era was one of mechanization, a supplanting of man's muscle by machines, and a development of interrelated craftsmanship in every field of production. Man's capacity to perform work doubled and tripled many times. With the advent of the combustion engine and electricity, coupled with the introduction of the assembly line, America entered its Second Industrial Revolution. Man's capacity to perform work increased a thousandfold. But this was only a prelude to the era of explosive technology that was to be ushered in mid-way of this century.

Whereas the age of mechanization and the subsequent development of the assembly line could be characterized as **skilled men** operating **skilled machines**, we crossed the threshold in the early '40's into the Third Industrial Revolution of **skilled machines** operating **skilled machines**. This, of course, is today's era, identified as that of automation-cybernation. The scope of this new revolution has not yet been envisioned and yet its effects, both in the way of production potential and displacement of men, have already been felt with devastating impact throughout the economy.

From the time of this nation's first beginnings to the present time, its technological history is one of developing better and better machines to produce goods and services. The broad picture that emerges is one of a nation with the crudest of tools which represented only 2 percent of the nation's productive capacity developing technologically to the present time when its tools and scientific know-how represent 98 percent of our work potential.

There is no need to cover with laborious detail the successive industrial revolutions marking our major technological advancements. What is of concern to us is the fact that a nation of people have not progressively been the beneficiaries of such improved technology, both as to greater economic security and as to gaining equity in the know-how and producing machinery itself. The disconcerting evidence is that in terms of solvency, in terms of security and in terms of ease of mind, the majority are worse off than their ancestors were a century and a half ago. And yet the potential to do work, as reflected in our current technology, could create an abundant life for each and every human being in our society.

Unfortunately, the average citizen from the earliest history of the nation has not been aware of what was transpiring to disadvantage him or he has been helpless to prevent what he saw happening. Certainly there were no constitutional safeguards to afford him economic protection.

When the individual shoemaker made the completed shoe himself, he knew the effort he had expended and was in a position to protect his own interests when he traded or sold his shoes. However, when he went to work at the shoe factory and now performed only one operation on the shoe and received wages for his day's work, he was at the mercy of the factory owner. Being relieved of the responsibilities of running his own business, it did not occur to him that he was not getting his rightful benefit from machine production, and further that he was not realizing any equity or ownership of the enterprise he was helping to build.

Shortage of Purchasing Power

Workers are the nation's consumers. Their ability to buy the nation's production is in direct ratio to the purchasing power they possess in the form of wages. Because they have not received wages proportionate to their contribution to production, an inevitable shortage of buying power has always periodically resulted. In the past, as is the case now, goods piled up and factories closed. How could workers buy the goods produced if their wages fell far short of that which they had produced? Or if they had to pay prices disproportionate to their wages? But then as now they accepted that the amounts they had been shortsuited were the rightful "profit" of owners who simply set up new factories to restart the same cycle.

History refers to such cycles as panics, depressions and recessions. They have all been characterized by unemployment, foreclosures, general anguish and suffering, and a people and their government being further burdened with taxes and indebtedness.

Starting with the panic of 1819, up to the present there has been a consistent pattern of major panics and depressions occurring approximately every 20 years.

The key to the understanding of periodic economic breakdowns is to understand that to the exact degree that privately owned and privately directed capitalism perfects its tools and science of production, to that exact degree there is a **surplus of manpower** and a **surplus of goods**. Because as machines and techniques are introduced into the field of production, the same amounts of products and services, and even greater amounts, can be produced with less workers, both skilled and unskilled.

Of course, if the economy had' been basically an equitable economy, the perfection of tools would have redounded in benefits proportionately to both the workers and the consumers. The workers would have needed to work less time for the same amount of wages because machines had simply removed the burden from men's backs, and the consumers in turn would have needed to pay less for both products and services because increased productivity had lessened the cost of all items on the market.

Private capitalism, however, has not, and does not, work that way. Instead of maintaining full employment but with less hours for each worker, men are laid off. Instead of prices for both goods and services being reduced because of labor-saving machines, prices are "administered" and the consumers forced to pay all the traffic will bear.

Perfection of the means of producing more efficiently under private capitalism, in its basic functioning, is nothing more nor less than a **compounding of profits and a compounding of assets for a minority gaining ever-increasing control over the entire economy**.

Exodus for All Small Operators

While most people are aware of the tremendous strides made in industry in the perfecting of both tools and technology, they are not so aware of the same strides in agriculture. However, it is in farming that the inherent flaws in the current system of production and distribution are so overwhelmingly evident. What shocks the person commencing to feel concern over what is happening to his nation is the spectre of tens of millions going to bed each night without proper nourishment, some ten million suffering from acute malnutrition, while at the same time the most basic producer of food is being driven out of business.

In 1830, 70 percent of the labor force was employed in agriculture to feed the population of the country. By 1880 the number had dropped to 50 percent and by 1930 it had dropped to 20 percent. Today only 8 percent of the population lives on the estimated 3.4 million farms now operating. But the further projection is that 2.4 percent of the present farms will be liquidated, largely through foreclosures, within the near future. As in monopolistic industry, the large corporate farms are driving the small operators out of the whole economy.

Although both small businesses and small farms are foredoomed, it is the elimination of the farmer that is making ghost towns of the rural hamlets and smaller cities. It is the small farmer going out of business that is taking the small rural businessman with him. Small grocery stores, clothing stores, and automobile agencies cannot exist without the purchases of many small farmers and their families. So the accelerated liquidation of all small farms means the accelerated liquidation of all rural businesses.

The small farmer and the small businessman, either as manufacturer or retailer, cannot compete with the advantages enjoyed by the monopolies. All share the same plight. All are slated to become outcasts of a monopolistic society.

And of course, the same fate lies in store for the larger number of workers, ultimately numbering in the tens of millions, who are displaced by an automated and cybernated society.

An Automated Society

What the nation must face up to now is that technologically it has come smack up against major turning point in machine production. It is the development and perfecting of electronic devices that coordinate and integrate all machine operations without the need of men to check or supervise the machine's performance. The far-reaching potential of this technological development, which lends itself to be applied to every aspect of our society, defies imagination.

There are countless technical books on the subject. These are for engineers. Our concern is just to grasp broadly the potential of the automated age, and most importantly to understand how it can be either a curse or a blessing to mankind.

Let us first give thought to the first introduction of automation. This was in the automotive industry and quite appropriately was called "Detroit Automation." It involved what is called the transfer machine which made possible the coupling of a series of machines into a single line of production so that successive operations were automatic and could be supervised from a central control system. No longer was it necessary for skilled men to operate and supervise independent machines.

There is no industry that has not been affected by this type of factory automation. Millions of men have been displaced by such automated machinery. The steel industry, the textile, the coal, the electrical field, the automotive, have had their work forces cut nearly **in half**, yet their productivity has risen in most cases over **fifty** percent. The story has always been the same: More products and less men to produce them. And with less men with wages, there has been less purchasing power to buy both the goods and the services available.

But wholesale displacement of production, or factory, workers is the lesser half of the automation picture. With the introduction of electronic computers, the amazing machine systems that have unlimited capability to both store and process data, machines have come into being that can supplant large areas of man's thinking and can perform not only more rapidly but more accurately. The scope of the performance of computers and data-communications systems is almost endless in application.

From a layman's standpoint, it is necessary to understand only the two basic functions of computers in order to get a glimpse into the potential that exists for making the machine the willing servant of mankind. The first function is that of storing information with the accompanying ability to retrieve any that may be desired instantly. It is now possible to store all the books of the world in one national computerized library and every home could extract data via electronic communication, either typed or visual. Of course, this must await actual realization, but it done.

However, already the whole approach to keeping records and statistics, and doing all types of research has been revolutionized. Computer installations already are being put to use in the legal and medical professions, in teaching and government. Wholesale replacement of clerical and supervising personnel in business and all aspects of industry is taking place by computer installation.

The other basic function of computers is as data processing systems. It is the computer in this role in conjunction with self-regulating machines that has opened the door not only on our whole adventure into space, but has also opened the door in the operating of entire industries with men needed only for purposes of maintenance. Through the principle of electronic "feed-back," all errors and deviations in performance will automatically correct themselves so that a single machine, or many machines, will continue to function in a predetermined or "programmed" manner.

In a basic sense, the ultimate in automation-cybernation is the integrating of machines so that they can digest data and direct decisions to other machines that operate automatically. This would make possible the complete systematizing and coordinating of entire enterprises. **It is now within the reach of man to set up one vast, integrated, national productive machine that would provide for all the material needs of all the people in the entire nation!**

Potential for Abundance

In short, this nation has crossed the threshold into an age of production and communication potential that not only could erase all poverty, illiteracy and disease from our midst, and could lift all grueling and repetitious drudgery from mankind's back, but that could usher in an era of such abundance in necessities and comforts as to create a virtual material paradise for the nation's entire citizenry. But it is not the conquering of man's material challenges that poses the greater triumph. It would be the freeing of mankind at last to confront his cultural and spiritual challenges.

In a later chapter we shall consider the technological potential that now exists, the television in conjunction with the computerized telephone that makes possible the bringing of government directly into each home and the full opportunity for the people to exercise absolute sovereignty in all decision-making in shaping their lives and culture.

In 1961, the Subcommittee on Unemployment and the Impact of Automation of the United States Congress conducted a comprehensive investigation into automation's effect on employment and the scope of its potential as to the nation's productive capability. Those testifying were the most knowledgeable men in the fields of electronics, computers, automation and cybernation. Out of that testimony came the conclusion that if the nation were to utilize its best technology-that which had already been engineered—only ten percent of the entire labor force would be needed to produce all that the nation then produced, including all that it shipped abroad. Since then giant strides have been made in all fields toward a greater perfection of technology. Yet even eight years ago it was estimated that each worker would have to work only four hours a week (ten percent of 40 hours) to accomplish the nation's production. Taking the technological capacity estimated by the Subcommittee and multiplying it by ten representing the entire labor force, we could come up with a Gross National Product approaching some eight to ten trillion dollars.

However, it is knowledge of doing things that is the real wealth of the nation. Whereas in the past it has been resources plus tools that counted in the providing of goods and services, it is now energy plus knowhow. In light of the fact that in chemistry and physics we have tapped into all-pervading energy, there is no limit to the energy available. Therefore it is our knowhow that reflects our real wealth. The **capability** to make computers, to erect atomic plants, to set up industrial enterprises, to build houses, cars, electrical appliances, and all the needs and comforts of life exceed all these tangible things. The know-how is our capability to **duplicate** innumerable times the existing wealth at any point in time.

Point of No Return

When we come to consider the new economic framework that must be brought into being, we will more adequately consider the technological potential existing. Right now we should appreciate that there is nothing wrong with automation or the entire evolutionary process of developing the most efficient ways in which to carry on a nation's production of both goods and services. On the other hand, we must recognize that there is much wrong with an economic system that gives a minority the despotic power of **owning, directing** and **benefiting** from such technology to the exclusion of the vast majority.

In terms of perfected technology and monopolistic control it could be said that the Great Depression of the 1930's signaled the point of no return for private capitalism. The unworkableness and criminality of the system reached a climax when producing machines throughout the nation came to a standstill, livestock were slaughtered and crops destroyed under the guise of decreasing "over-production"—all at a time when one-third of the entire population were ill-fed, ill-clothed and ill-housed.

Many Americans are alive today who witnessed and endured the insufferable conditions that were all part of that period. Not only were there wholesale evictions of millions from their homes, their businesses, but the magnitude of the unemployed reached the staggering number of 15,000,000 jobless Americans.

Only a prolonged orgy of indebtedness and three bloody wars, one in which the nation is still embroiled, have prevented complete collapse of the whole socio-economic system. It is at this point that we want to consider the primary mechanisms that have served to perpetuate and bail out private capitalism, and in a follow-up chapter to consider the serious side effects of the system itself.

Chapter 12

BAILING OUT THE "SYSTEM"

B Y THE TURN of the last century, the larger part of the nation's natural wealth had become lodged in the hands of a small segment of the population and the safety valve of virgin territory no longer served to offset the inequities of an economic system premised on imbalances.

Broadly speaking, it could be stated that four other areas came to serve as "stabilizers" in preventing the whole economic structure from collapsing under the weight of its unworkability and injustice.

While they are interrelated and interdependent, they could be listed as:

1. Indebtedness
2. Bureaucratic welfarism
3. Imperialistic investments and foreign aid.
4. Embroilment in wars.

To the exact degree that the people of this nation have been denied both their rightful purchasing and their rightful equity in the economy, the foregoing mechanisms have come into play to bail out private capitalism. We should understand at least in essence the role each has played.

Indebtedness

In a subsequent chapter, there will be a more comprehensive coverage of private banking and the disastrous impact it has had on the nation's economy since the inception of this nation. Only a few paragraphs will suffice here in identifying debt, both public and private, as the chief mechanism for preventing the complete collapse of the economy throughout the nation's history.

We have already considered the circumstance that periodically private capitalism has created artificial gluts of goods by the very fact that the "profits" extracted out of production simply reflected the underpayments to the workers in wages and the overcharges to the consumers in prices. The perfection of the tools of production only compounded the inability of the people to buy what the machines could produce. Both unemployment and lack of purchasing power were the dual characteristics of each successive panic and depression.

It is with this background that the private bankers, or debt-merchants, came into the picture. A people who were unable to buy what they in the accumulate had produced were given no choice but to place liens against their future work in order to buy that which was already piled up in unmovable inventory. Incredible as it seems in viewing our economic history in retrospect, the major strides that the nation has made in harnessing machines to do work has resulted in a progressive picture of greater and greater indebtedness. Certainly it is strange that the imbecility of such economics should not have been long ago detected and discarded.

But the imbecility of indebtedness, with all the evils of interest, as a means of artificially creating purchasing power is only one of the diabolical ramifications of a nation's money supply being under the control of private bankers. Beside deflating and inflating the money supply, thus destroying additional purchasing power of the people and causing wholesale foreclosures, the private money-merchants create "fountain pen" credit by which they capitalize industry and buy up the nation's resources.

To grasp in its most basic essence the role of private banking, particularly in terms of indebtedness, is to recognize that the nation has always had two kinds of dollars. One has been represented by work and was an earned dollar. The other was manufactured by the banks and was an unearned dollar.

Private banking, with all its myriad forms of interest bearing indebtedness has been the camouflaged handmaiden of private capitalism, providing the enforced expedient by which an entire citizenry and its government have mortgaged their future working capacity in order to buy that which they have already produced. Progressively, they have pyramided their indebtedness in direct ratio to the unearned claims that profiteers have siphoned out of the economy. Inescapable is the fact that private capitalism is a system predicated on indebtedness and bondage.

We will have much more to say on the subject in a later chapter.

Bureaucratic Welfarism

If there is one truism that is subscribed to by most people, it is the best government is the least government. Automatically, most people rebel against all aspects of government dictation and government welfarism. In particular are they fed up with the endless forms, decrees and red tape emanating from a whole gamut of non-producing and wasted bureaucrats. What the average citizen really finds intolerable is the mushrooming taxes that he must pay in order to keep Big Brother in operation.

In the past 10 years Federal taxes have increased 71.3 percent, local taxes have increased 120.5 percent and State taxes have increased 260.9 percent. Today, in the spring of 1969, the total tax burden of the average citizen in the United States is the staggering amount of **34 percent** of his salary.

What the citizens of the nation have not clearly recognized is that Big Government with all its attendant bureaucracy and taxation has all come about because the inequities and malfunctions of the economic system have created the vacuums into which government could step. Along with the private and public debt to the private bankers, government has simply stepped into the picture to care of those disadvantaged and those excluded from the economy.

When the worker becomes unemployed, he has no other place to turn than to government for his unemployment checks. The same is true for the farmer and small businessman who must get assistance in the form of subsidies. For the tens of millions precluded from any rightful purchasing claim against the economy, those enduring poverty and numbered amongst the unemployed, there is no alternative but the pittances in relief checks or outright receipt of "commodities."

The ironical circumstance exists that while the most destitute and unemployed, including the small farmer and businessman, are begrudged such government hand-outs, the rich and their monopolies are also the recipients of hand-outs that are not so labeled. Relief to the poor is no more the subsidy of bureaucratic government than oil depletion allowances, tax-exempt bonds and the hundred and one cost-plus defense contracts. The latter are carried out, of course, under the guise of "sound" business practices. In reality the only difference is that the poor have to accept their subsidies from a position of weakness while the rich extract their subsidies from positions of privileged domination.

Burgeoning government, all forms of welfarism and subsidies, and the whole structure of confiscatory and privileged taxation have all come about because of an economic system that did not give each and every citizen his rightful claims against the producing capacity of the nation.

Private capitalism has not only created a circumstance, as now existing, of 30 to 40 million living in poverty but to date only one out of every three of those are even able to obtain welfare. Most intolerable is the tragedy of some 10 million who are the victims of acute malnutrition, a polite name for starvation.

Even the most ardent apologists for private capitalism must find it difficult to defend an economic system within which children die from lack of food when public shelves are overloaded and farmers are paid billions of dollars to let land lie idle, not to mention the billions of dollars of foodstuffs rotting in government storehouses.

The assessment must be made that Big Brother government grows and is necessary to the exact degree that the nation's economic system is both inadequate and unjust. Citizens who are economically solvent and prosperous are citizens who will not tolerate either government bureaucracy or government dictation.

Like the nation's debt-merchants, government has extended its power beyond all the bounds of legitimate service into a role of unwarranted authority. In this sense, both are non—producing overlords.

Imperialistic Investments and Foreign Aid

Imperialistic investments have always been a prime objective of the monopolistic power structures in our economy—taking their unearned capital to foreign countries to start the merry game of exploiting the hard work of other human beings just as they have done in America. This, of course, meant dealing with the military and political dictatorships in those lands, who were insensitive to the well-being of their own citizens.

Behind all the efforts of "free trade," "low tariffs" and "reciprocal agreements" has been the clandestine activity of the exploiters in one land agreeing to and encouraging the exploitation of the citizens of another.

The key to an understanding of foreign investments is the fact that the hundreds of billions that have been invested in foreign countries did not come from some distant planet. These investments are the accumulated "capital" extorted out of this nation's economy and reflect the wage shortages and over-pricing of all the people. While there is some substance to the contention that accumulated capital re-invested in our own nation furnishes new jobs and stimulates the economy, there is no validity to this contention when the unearned capital of the monopolies is invested abroad. Estimates in recent years are that 4 out of every 5 dollars of the giant monopolies' investment profits are invested in foreign enterprises.

Foreign aid is another factor in siphoning off purchasing power from the American people by taxation.

Since World War II, the taxpayers' dollars have gone to foreign countries in the way of foreign aid exceeding 125 billion dollars. No American would object to assisting the down-trodden of other lands if we as a nation could afford it and the people in need in foreign countries actually got the help. On the other hand, it is difficult to understand why foreigners should get preference to Americans in the same dire need.

Belatedly, however, the hidden reason behind the whole worldwide squanderbust is uncovering itself. It has nothing basic to do with help to distressed foreigners or the promotion of democratic governments in other lands. It has everything to do with how to tax the people so that the overloaded warehouses of the monopolists could be emptied.

Under the guise of military necessity, and Christian charity, it was calculated the people would not protest the billions collected in taxes to be sent to foreign countries. At the same time, it was cunningly concluded that American taxpayers would not deduce that the larger amount of such extorted money would be directed to the purchase of the over-production in this country to buy the goods that the taxpayers in the accumulate produced but couldn't buy.

Time and event are slowly but surely revealing the 125-billion-dollar gimmick for what it is-another colossal cover-up for the unworkability of our debt-money structure.

The most serious aspect of all foreign loans, foreign investments and foreign government aid is that they have been but a prelude to military commitments and pledges of American blood and treasure.

Embroilment in Wars

Few are the people of this nation who are insensitive to the brutality of war with its attendant killing and human suffering. In this age of electronics, the horrors of war are brought right into the living room of the preponderance of American homes. Each night, viewers of television are brought into direct proximity with the dead and dying, the destruction of homes and countryside, and the helpless refugees, uprooted and bewildered.

There is no need for conjecture and distant speculation. The barbarism of war impinges with full impact on our souls and consciousness. Even the most callous must feel that there is something senseless in killing and wanton destruction in order to resolve the differences between peoples. You don't help people by destroying their homeland. You don't preserve life by extinguishing it.

But being horrified and sickened by the ghastly realities of war, and praying for peace is one thing. It is another to face up to the harsh fact that treaties, military commitments and the "attacks" that inevitably occur are the premeditated designs of economic and political forces entrenched in power who profit while the young die. What must be faced is that all the exhortations to patriotism, all the goals of "making the world safe for democracy," and all the pleadings to slay some "monster" who will devour our nation are but camouflage to veil the economic and political considerations that underlie our embroilments.

The ordinary citizens of every land are no different from the ordinary citizens of our own nation. They seek, as we seek, the opportunity to live in peace, to raise families and to try to realize the most satisfying life commensurate with their nation's capabilities. The ordinary people of all countries, especially those conscripted to kill and destroy, are simply pitted against each other through artificially created hate and manipulated events. Wars don't just happen. They are made to happen.

During the latter part of 1967 a book was published that should make every American take a most serious look at the nation's embroilment in wars. The name of the book is "Report From Iron Mountain," published by Dial Press, and outside of a short foreword, it is written anonymously.

For those who may not know of the book, or at least may not have read it, let it be explained that the book purports to cover the findings of a Special Study Group, made up of fifteen members of a cross-section of professional men throughout the nation, who were commissioned to "determine accurately and realistically, the nature of the problems that would confront the United States if and when a condition of 'permanent peace' should arrive, and to draft a program for dealing with this contingency."

The foreword covers the development that when the Report was completed it was suppressed, both by the Special Study Group and by the government interagency committee to which it had been submitted, and that the publishing of the Report was the result of one member's deciding that he didn't want to be a party to the suppression. It goes on to state that the Group as a whole feared that release of the Report would he too explosive politically and too disconcerting to all who would read it.

No one knows, of course, whether this Special Study Group actually existed or that a literal Report was made and really exists. Perhaps the whole book is merely a hypothetical presentation. This is irrelevant.

What is relevant is that the findings simply confirm in considerable analytical detail a harsh fact that has been known to the enlightened for many years. **Wars are not only a stabilizing factor to offset the inequities of private capitalism but peace can never be truly attained until the built-in evils of private capitalism are eradicated.**

While the book uses as its central the premise that war is itself "the principal basis of organization on which all modern societies are constructed," and presents a convincing case respecting the economic, political, scientific and cultural ramifications of war-oriented societies, it fails to make any mention of mass indebtedness, or foreign investment, or the abundance of land in our early history, as other instruments for bailing out private capitalism. However, what the book has to say about war being a mandatory function to periodically take care of **surplus goods** and **surplus manpower** is deadly in its accuracy.

Agonizing as it must be to mothers, wives and sweethearts to have their menfolk thousands of miles away dying to keep a nation's economy intact, the reality of the conclusion must be faced. From an agrarian society to a highly technological society the nation has passed through a calculated history of wars designed to take care of the gross inefficiencies and injustices of private capital. Human suffering and death itself are the penalties or price paid in order to maintain an economic order that has thrived on disservice to the majority.

It has been wars during the last fifty years that have served primarily in bailing out the system. During this period of time, this nation has become a stained-in-blood economy in four different brutal wars. It is not necessary to debate the war objectives in order to pinpoint the fact that without the artificial stimulus war gave to the economy, there would have been a breakdown of economic structure. No one can ignore the circumstance that while human blood was being spilled in Flanders and on beaches in Normandy and on Pork Chop Hill in Korea and in the jungles of Vietnam, the economy was booming on the homefront.

Wars simply divert a nation's productive machinery to producing war materiel, thus reducing a glutted inventory of peacetime goods which people do not have the purchasing power to buy, and at the same time increasing the purchasing power of the people through the wages and salaries of war-oriented production.

Coupled with this achievement is the putting of the nation's surplus workers into uniform to be shipped out of the land and thus out of the increasing labor pool.

Of course, it is a field day for the debt-merchants every time. And backbreaking debt becomes tolerable when wars are labelled "patriotic" and in the name of "liberty" and in the "defense of freedom." Congressmen seem to find it impossible to vote against war appropriations. "Backing the boys," they call it, but re-election may be assured for them by their supplying constituents with highpaying defense jobs, and shepherding lucrative war contracts into their own areas. At the same time, workers find no reason to oppose higher taxes and deeper indebtedness when their paychecks are doubled. Any opposition to any war is met by the propagandists with cries of "Slackerism!", "Cowardice!" and "Aid to the enemy!"

However, a day of reckoning had to come. The built-in flaws, the injustices, of private capitalism would so compound that the "stabilizing" mechanisms in our society would be exposed as nothing but diabolical expedients for patching up, and holding together, a socio-economic system unworkable from the beginning.

However, we do not indict individuals. It is the system itself, the "business-is-business," greed-encouraging, materialistic system of private capitalism that blinds and desensitizes its practitioners, loosening their moral fibre—for the only way to succeed in this system is by the accumulation of money together with the ability to exercise power over others.

There is now an ironical development. The very technology— mechanization to cybernation—that has been filling the coffers of power-hungry profiteers with more and more spoils, is the same technology that is about to undo the game of unearned profit-taking. Not only has indebtedness increased at a faster rate than the rate of productivity, but at the same time technology has created more goods and more unemployed than manipulated wars can destroy.

The final *coup de grace* administered by advanced technology is the creation of such weapons of war that for the first time those who profit by wars are no longer safe themselves. Nuclear weaponry is no respecter of persons, with or without garnered wealth. Wars, as chief "stabilizers" of a debt-economy, have turned upon their manipulators.

If there is one major lesson to be derived from socio-economic systems predicated on exploitation and disadvantaging the majority, it is that both the exploiters and the exploited are losers in the ultimate. There are no winners when the chips are down.

True peace for our nation and for the world can only come when an economic order is brought about that is not dependent on wars, and all the other negative gimmicks for artificially resuscitating a nation with antidotes that only further sicken the nation and its people.

Chapter 13

SIDE EFFECTS

THIS HAS BEEN the insatiable thrust of private capitalism to maximize profits and concentrate minority ownership that has given rise to so many serious side effects, not only involving indeterminable hundreds of billions of dollars in waste of resources and human effort, including both physical and mental injury to the entire citizenry, but also the even greater crime of precluding full use of the nation's capacity to do the things that could have been done. There is no way of making a true assessment. However, we need to have some identification of the major side effects of private capitalism.

In considering these side effects we are not now concerning ourselves with the instruments for bailing out the economic system which we considered in the last chapter. We are concerning ourselves with the waste in humans and wealth within the operation of the economic system itself.

Seductive Advertising

First, there is the whole area of advertising, accounting for roughly one-third of the total price paid by consumers. Advertising bears no resemblance to a constructive role of informing the buying public of comparative values in a competitive marketplace. As practiced in current times, it is a multi-billion-dollar seductive gimmick to force and inveigle customers to buy beyond their purchasing ability. It involves all the come-ons of trading stamps, contests, trips to Paris, all the countless brochures and lithographed boxes, all the radio and TV commercials, and the entertainment programs themselves.

It is estimated that the packaging industry alone costs in the neighborhood of 20 billion dollars a year. Perhaps the disproportionate cost is best understood in light of the fact that a soap firm wishing to change the advertising on its container threw away its already packaged product because the cost of the box exceeded the worth of the contents.

There is no need to amplify the nature of advertising. Ninety percent borders on outright misrepresentation and is based either on sensuality or on fear. Lost to most people is the fact that the slapstick comedy, trashy shows and political propaganda are all underwritten by the buyers of products and services. Not only are the buyers forced to pay for entertainment which they do not care for, but at the same time they are, through advertising, underwriting their own propagandizing as to the "glories of the free enterprise" system.

No aspect of our economic system has so devastatingly misused and corrupted the English language as advertising. The finest words, with high aesthetic or superlative connotations, have been blatantly used to describe deodorants, candy bars, sporting equipment, hair spray and the most trivial items used by the average household.

In a constructive economy, advertising must be dissociated from all fields of entertainment. Advertising would fall strictly in the field of education with products and services described to the public by engineers, designers and creators unbeholden to the actual producers or sellers. This will be considered when we give thought later to an economy in which this approach would be a natural function.

"On the Job Slaughter"

While advertising forces the people to pay upwards of one-third of their purchasing power without getting anything of intrinsic value in return, it is injury and death to millions of human beings that is a much more serious side effect of private capitalism. What we want to consider briefly are a number of aspects which underscore this built in disregard for life itself. In so doing, we should bear in mind that preservation of life is the most elementary purpose of organized society. A society that fails to protect and preserve life is little worthy of respect and obedience by its members.

Unfortunately it is only when a tragedy like the West Virginia mine disaster occurs (November, 1968 in which 78 men lost their lives) that the average American gives any thought to how callously dispensable are human beings in the functioning of our economy. He then gets momentary glimpses into the preciousness of life, particularly in terms of those who are deprived of their loved ones. However, he is largely oblivious to the fact that life throughout our present private-capitalistic system has been made so cheap and expendable.

Let us start with the West Virginia mine tragedy. When auto industry critic, Ralph Nader, spoke at a news conference in South Bend, Indiana and later to a student group at the University of Notre Dame on November 20, 1968, he stated that the mining industry's safety program "is medieval and legislators from mining states represent the coal industry, not the people." He went on to state, "The mining industry is the second most hazardous in terms of 'black lung disease.' One out of every two miners contracts it."

In broadening our scope to all industry, we are in for some gruesome statistics. Our information comes from a U. S. Labor Dept. pamphlet called, "On the Job Slaughter—A National Shame."

> In the next 8 minutes, a man or woman in America will be killed needlessly . . . 148 others will be disabled, many of them maimed for life . . . not slaughtered on the highways . . . not victims of fire or flood . . . but cut down on the job, in the prosaic work-a-day business of earning their daily bread.

The annual figures are shocking: Every twelve months 14,000 to 15,000 Americans are killed on the job . . . More than 2,000,000 are disabled by occupational accidents . . . . Over 500,000 disabled by occupational disease . . . . More than 7,000,000 are injured.

Incredible as it may seem, it is estimated that 80 percent of the entire labor force works without any occupational health service and with very little effective protection against conventional safety hazards. Thousands of workers every year die slow, often agonizing deaths from the effects of asbestos, beryllium, carbon monoxide, coal dust, cotton dust, cancer-causing chemicals, dyes, unusual fuels, pesticides, radiation and other occupational hazards such as heat, vibration or noise.

According to the Committee on Environmental Quality of the Federal Council for Science & Technology there are more than 6,000,000 workers and possibly as many as 16,000,000 who are now exposed to noise unsafe for hearing.

What should register with the average American is that our private capitalistic system creates two conditions resulting in the foregoing intolerable and needless sacrifice in health and life. One is that the small operator is so pressed to remain in competition that he cannot afford all the safety precautions. On the other hand, the industrial oligarchies and conglomerates are so geared to profits and power that the mighty dollar outweighs basic humane considerations of the people involved in their employ.

It is pertinent to note that the most vociferous opposition to health and safety legislation comes from such groups as the United States Chamber of Commerce, the National Association of Manufacturers and the Association of General Contractors. This is just added confirmation that humans are dispensable products within the economic framework so that bigger and bigger profits can accrue to the few who own and direct the economy.

On-the-job slaughter is only one side of the coin. The very same controllers of industry who are callous toward the health and life of their workers are ones who are responsible for the major part of the built-in obsolescence in all products, which in turn are the cause of millions of crippling accidents both in the home and on the highway. It is again the same story of an economic system that makes the increase of profits paramount in its operation instead of the improving of human beings.

There is not an American who is not aware that every time he and his family get into their car and a trip, they are placing their lives in danger. While it is true that reckless driving, especially by those under the influence of alcohol, is responsible for a large share of the accidents and deaths on the nation's highways, sheer neglect and refusal on the part of the auto industry to build a safe car are the real cause of much needless killing. It is now estimated, at the present rate of automobile accidents, that one out of every two Americans will be killed or hospitalized eventually by an automobile crash unless we do something about it.

Americans show more horror and alarm over the number of persons killed in riots than over the wholesale slaughter on our highways. Yet during the past three years (1966-1968), there have been only 360 deaths in all the riots less than **three** days' toll of all those killed in automobile accidents.

Crime and Drugs

We would be remiss if we didn't consider crime as a specific side effect of the over-all economy. Each year, crime accounts for an estimated 40 billion dollars in property loss in addition to the loss of human lives. The most shocking aspect of the alarming increase in crime is that over 50 % of all major crime is committed by teenagers. Not only is it not safe to go out on the nation's highways, but it is unsafe to walk after dark on one's own familial' streets or even to be in one's home.

There is much moralizing about a lack of proper family background, but in the majority of cases, the real problem is one of economics. Mothers are forced to work along with fathers in the day-to-day grind of paying inflationary prices and spiraling taxes which is just too much in trying to maintain a stable and harmonious home. When we give thought to the ghettos of the nation, where millions are forced to live in the most deplorable conditions, when we give thought to the violence of war with an entire nation geared to death instead of life, and when we give thought to the over-riding motivation of the economic system which is to deprive others of that which belongs to them, we cannot escape indicting private capitalism itself for orienting and forcing people into crime.

Directly related to crime are the billions of dollars in correctional institutions, prisons and the whole spectrum of court actions which deal with punishments and lawsuits. Again, as is so true respecting other aspects and side effects of the economy, it is not the momentary waste that is the most exacting. It is the cost in wasted human lives that is the most tragic.

Running parallel with crime as a side effect of our economy is the whole field of drug addiction, not only involving morphine and heroin but involving the wholesale use of sedatives and an annual consumption of nine to ten billion dollars in alcohol

When we consider the costs in terms of the people incapacitated, the lives broken and the endless hospital and doctor care necessary, the cost in the actual drugs and alcohol themselves is the lesser burden.

It is conservatively estimated that throughout the nation, 20 percent of the people are either under some type of mental care or in need of it. Here, again, we are compelled to chalk up against the socio-economic system the main responsibility for creating the tensions, frustrations and stresses that unanchor people and cause them to break under an overload of pressure.

Poisoning the Environment

Finally, we must mention, as a specific side effect of the economic system, the wholesale pollution of air, land and water which can be charged up to industrial disregard for the health of society. Hundreds of millions of tons of pollutants have been indiscriminately dumped into the rivers and lakes, and poured into the atmosphere. The criminality of such wholesale pollution is underscored by the fact that science and technology have ways to prevent it.

There is no measuring stick by which to determine the overall damage done to plant and life along with human life. Not only is the crippling process of pollution a prolonged agony, the utterly thoughtless or callous interference with delicate ecological balances not only may require years to evaluate and correct, but if the trend is not turned, an environment will be created that will ultimately be unsafe for all forms of life.

If one were to draw a line under just the side effects of our socio-economic system and we have only dealt sketchily with some of the more obvious—the amount would be sufficient in itself to under-write the complete elimination of poverty, provide for full education for every child in the nation, provide for full medical care for every human being in the nation, and there would still be billions left over to add cultural values to the society.

Chapter 14

OUTCASTS OF THE "SYSTEM"

NO ADEQUATE analysis of private capitalism can be made without noting the exclusion of entire races of people from the socio-economic-political framework. For both the black man and the red man, there is a consistent history of being outcasts of the society. While the black people's existence can be identified as sheer slavery, for the Indians it has been the concentration camp in the form of enforced isolation on reservations. It is impossible to portray the emotional suffering, along with the brutality, heaped upon both these races of human beings. Even the best of full books cannot do it with any true measure of hardships and indignities endured. There is an Indian saying, "Don't try to judge a man until you have walked three moons in his moccasins." Only the red man, or the black man, himself knows the tortuous road he has traveled from the earliest beginnings of this nation. It must be noted that the Indians were here when the first colonizers arrived, and that the first load of black slaves landed at Charleston, S.C. in 1619, one year before the Plymouth colony was founded.

Up to the Civil War, neither the Constitution nor the laws of white society recognized the Negro as a human being. While the 13th, 14th, and 15th Amendments declared the liberation of the black people, their freedom was in name only. Up to the present time, they have constantly been at the beck and call of a white racist society which has given them only the most menial and degrading employment, at the same time denying them the education necessary to the improvement of their own circumstances.

With the first organizations on their behalf, commencing in the early 1900's, up to 1954 with the Supreme Court ruling on school integration, the black people were primarily involved in getting legal affirmation of their equal status as citizens. With the highest court nullifying the doctrine of "equal but separate," the Civil Rights movement came into being demanding inclusion into other areas of public accommodations. Success to date has largely been confined to the elimination of Jim Crowism.

Whereas the parks, lunch counters and buses finally if grudgingly made room for him, the capitalistic system had no room for the Negro when he sought jobs, decent housing and adequate educational facilities for his children. He was then confronting an economic system of planned scarcity wherein there already wasn't enough for white citizens. Consequently there has arisen the white "backlash," the "black power" issue and all the ill-feeling between the races.

The current goals of the Civil Rights movement do not spell out freedom for the black people because it seeks integration into an unjust economic-political system in which the bulk of the non-black Americans already are, and have been, ruthlessly disserviced. Fortunately, many black leaders recognize the entrapment involved behind promotions as "black capitalism." Of course, black people should not be condemned for steps that alleviate their suffering or condition. However, they should recognize that what they are doing is simply elevating themselves into the area which is occupied by the vast majority of whites who only in lesser degree are the victims of the handful that own and direct the entire "system."

The perspective that is needed is that from the beginning the private capitalistic society has been a slave society for all its inhabitants. Within that slave society, the Negro and the Indian have been super-slaves.

No one race of human beings can be truly free until freedom is universal for all races, until there is **human equality**. The dignity of any person comes from his proportionate share of power in the whole of society. His acceptability is then automatic.

Chapter 15

AT THE MERCY OF DEBT-MERCHANTS

O F ALL the built-in flaws of our economic system, the ramifications of money and credit are the least comprehended. Yet, without a basic understanding of the whole private banking complex, there can be no working grasp of the capitalistic structure. The tentacles of the banking octopus reach into every cranny and crossroads in this nation. There is not a man, woman or child who escapes the direct effects of its economic strangulation.

It is one of the paradoxes of civilization that money is the one thing that is needed, and used, by more people than anything else, while it is at the same time, the least understood by them. There is no object more desperately sought for every minute of a person's life. Man will labor until aching muscles prevent sleep, he will put his life at stake, and he will steal and commit murder in order to acquire it. How strange that he evinces such little interest in understanding **what** money is, **how** it is created, and **who** controls the amount in circulation!

The answer, of course, lies in the fact that the average citizen has been conditioned to accept that the whole subject of money is too complex for his feeble brain to comprehend. He is unaware that the complexities and mysteries enshrouding the money question, and banking generally, have been promoted with premeditated design that the economic and financial enslavement of all might go undetected.

This is not to say that all bankers, especially the employees of the banking business, are themselves dishonest, or conscious destroyers of the will. It is to say that a monetary system, now so widespread as to be unquestioningly accepted, has been deliberately fostered, promoted and put over through the years by persons obsessed by the desire for personal power and profit, coupled with a complete indifference to the well-being of the rest of mankind. They have capitalized on the ordinary man's innate honesty and credulity to where the philosophy of the unscrupulous has become generally accepted as the right one, the respectable one, the desirable one.

Belatedly, the people must awaken to the realization that there cannot be any social reform, any ability for the citizenry as a whole to purchase all that the nation can produce, without fundamental monetary reform. A sovereign people who want to enjoy the full fruits of their hard work, who want to see their children free from needless indebtedness, and who want to build a nation commensurate with its technological potential must break the power of the nation's private debt-merchants.

It is sheer folly and blindness to seek economic well-being and social justice without confronting four-square the unyielding barrier of an archaic money supply.

The first enlightenment that must come to the people is that the private banking system of the present operates on the same fallacious principle as that of its progenitor, the 17th century goldsmith bankers. These were the private bankers who did largely all the banking of Western Europe. It was they who accidentally discovered the ruse of "fractional reserve" lending. Up the centuries it was to serve as the foundation for all private banking.

The goldsmiths were the custodians of gold. Those who owned the "precious" metal brought it to them for safe keeping. For each amount of gold deposited the goldsmiths gave the depositor a receipt which could be presented at any time and the amount of gold withdrawn. However, owners of the gold found that it was easier to exchange the receipts themselves in conducting their business than to disturb the gold in the vaults of the goldsmiths. In fact, only a very small percentage ever came to actually redeem their receipts.

Consequently the receipts circulated as "money" with no thought, or suspicion, by either buyer or seller, as to lack of any gold backing.

It was this circumstance that led the goldsmith bankers to the cunning and deceptive principle of "fractional reserve" banking. If the larger number of those who possessed the receipts for the deposited gold did not come in and claim their actual gold, what prevented the goldsmiths from loaning out the depositor's gold to others? In fact, what prevented the goldsmiths from writing out receipts for which no gold even existed? Who would be the wiser as long as they, the goldsmiths, simply maintained in their vaults sufficient gold to meet the claims of the small number who did present their receipts for gold payment?

This is exactly what the goldsmiths proceeded to do. They commenced **to manufacture** money, issuing receipts that neither had any gold backing nor were backed by either goods or services. They simply used the depositor's gold, not their own, as a fractional reserve against which to create fictitious receipts to be loaned out in the form of interest-bearing debt. Thus was born the **fractional reserve system** of private banking.

There is a long evolving history of private banking from the time of the goldsmiths to the Federal Reserve System of this Twentieth Century. However, it is a consistent history of private bankers using a deceptive form of "reserves" upon which they could increase manifold the money supply by the simple expedient of manufacturing "money" or "credit". More serious is the fact that all such artificial purchasing power has been put into circulation in the form of debt—obligating the people and their government with perpetual interest-bearing liens against both property and future labor.

The power to expand the money supply automatically carried with it the power to contract the supply. Thus, the power to inflate and deflate the amount of money has consistent given the private bankers the power to destroy the purchasing value of money, affect the price of every product and service, concentrate the assets of the nation in the hands of a minority, and arbitrarily cause depressions at will.

It was this power that Mayer Amschel Rothschild, the founder of the notorious Rothschild International Bankers, referred to when he boasted, "Permit me to issue and control the money of a nation, and I do not care who makes its laws." He knew, as he and his five sons so devastatingly proved, that no people, not even government itself, can go contrary to the dictates of those who control a nation's money supply.

History reveals a constant struggle by governments and their citizens to limit the power wielded by private bankers. So powerful have the bankers been, and so beholden have governments been to the bankers that at no time has a major nation been successful in setting up an honest and adequate money system that was solely under the jurisdiction of the sovereign people.

Unfortunately, it has always been the ignorance of the people and the supine indifference of their representatives and government that have permitted a minority to usurp the issuance and control of money—a function that belongs exclusively and absolutely to the people through their government.

Space is far too short in one chapter, or for that matter in a book, to delve into the chronological history of money and banking in this nation. However, we should first note that the framers of the Constitution did specifically intent that the power to control the nation's money should be retained in the hands of the people through the Congress. Article I, Section 8, Part 5 of the Constitution states, "Congress shall have power to coin money, regulate the value thereof, and of foreign coin." While only the word "coin" was used, because there were no banks of issue at the time, the Supreme Court has upheld the proposition that "whatever power there is over the currency is vested in the Congress."

The extension of banking control over the economies of all nations has been simply the process of bankers securely entrenched in one nation extending credit, or making their hoarded wealth available, to other nations. Invariably, this process has been the most effective in the case of underdeveloped nations or in the time of governments caught in the throes of war. So it was with our own nation. While the colonists saw the wisdom of issuing their own sovereign money, they were prohibited from doing so by the tyrannical government of George III. By the time they had won their independence, they were at the mercy of both foreign credit and American speculators who owned the main indebtedness of the new nation.

Within two years after the adoption of the Constitution in 1791, our own nation was placed in the clutches of private banking. It was engineered by Alexander Hamilton and the international financiers for whom he was spokesman. It was accomplished by the enactment of the First National Bank Act which gave birth, with the very inception of our Republic to the deceitful philosophy that the only "sound" money is debt-money.

Unsuspectingly, the nation had agreed to turn over to the private bankers the nation's bonds, or credit of the whole citizenry, as a "funding" of the existing debt, then allowing the bankers to issue bank notes on the government bonds. Not only was the power to control the amount of money in circulation placed in private hands but to them was extended the privilege of collecting interest on both the government bonds and the new "money" which they created in the form of loans.

Thus was born the gigantic piece of monetary chicanery that holds sway to the present. Stripped to stark nakedness, it stands exposed as a monument to mankind's naiveté in protecting both his hard work and the product of his labor and what does such major deceit encompass.

It encompasses the acceptance that while a nation's bonds—secured by the whole nation—and the private citizen' assets and working capacity, are sufficient for the private banks to issue money and make loans, those same

bonds, assets and working capacity are not sufficient for a sovereign people themselves to put money directly into circulation without incurring any debt or without paying any vampiristic tribute called interest.

Founding Fathers Grapple With Private Banking

For over 175 years a developing nation was to be burdened with needless debt and have both its industry and commerce servile to the manipulations of debt-merchants. However, our forefathers were by no means unmindful of what was happening. In van, they pitted their opposition to the private banking interest which wielded too much power even in the nation's infancy.

Consider the reaction of Thomas Jefferson who authored the Declaration of Independence, was the Republic's third President, and was the nation's staunchest pleader for a democratic society. In a letter to John Taylor, he had this to say:

> I believe that banking institutions are more dangerous to our liberties than standing armies. Already they have raised up a money aristocracy that has set the Government at defiance. The issuing power should be taken from the banks and restored to the Government to whom it properly belongs.

Equally vehement in underscoring the fallacies and dangers inherent in private control of the nation's money supply was President John Adams. His reactions, summed up in a letter to Thomas Jefferson have been echoed up the entire history of our nation by those who have investigated the money question. Terse and to the point, Adams wrote:

All the perplexities, confusion and distress in America arise, not from want of honor or virtue, so much as from downright ignorance of the nature of coin, credit and circulation.

An ironical twist of events found Jefferson President of the nation at the outbreak of the War of 1812. So dependent was the nation for its money supply on the private bankers that he was compelled to acquiesce to the chartering of the Second Bank of the United States, twenty years later,

President Andrew Jackson vetoed the bill that would have renewed the charger which expired in 1836. It is well to note that under President Jackson's tenure, the nation was free of all debt. Under no administration, before or after, was the nation to be free of needless interest-bearing indebtedness.

President Jackson, along with Jefferson and Adams, recognized the stupidity of a sovereign nation making itself beholden to private bankers for its supply of money. Why should a nation that had just won its political freedom become subservient to financial despots and thus make a mockery of economic freedom? In his farewell address of March 4, 1837, he minced no words in making this indictment of the privately owned central bank of issue:

> In the hands of this formidable power, thus organized, was also placed unlimited dominion over the amount of circulating medium, giving it the power to regulate the value of property and the fruits of labor in every quarter of the union, and to bestow prosperity or bring ruin upon any city or section of the country as might best comport with its own interest or policy . . . . Yet, if you had not conquered, the government would have passed from the hands of the many to the hands of the few, and this organized money power from its secret conclave would have dictated the choice of your highest officers and compelled you to make peace or war, as

best suited their wishes. The forms of your government might for a time have remained, but its living spirit would have departed from it.

President Andrew Jackson had made a heroic gesture in trying to liberate the nation from the stultifying and exploitive power of private bankers but history must record it only as a gesture. He provided no sound alternative. Government deposits were placed in State banks which in turn used the public credit in a splurge of reckless lending that led to widespread indebtedness and bank failures. Thus ensued the panic of 1837 with its attendant foreclosures and inflated prices. It was the first of the major money panics that were to afflict the nation.

Lincoln's "Greenbacks"

Of all the outstanding men who make up the best of American history, Abraham Lincoln perhaps more clearly than anyone understood how wrong it is for anyone except government to issue the nation's money. He did more than indict the unscrupulous private bankers and challenge their unchecked power to place a whole nation in bondage and famish its people. He courageously gave the nation the only honest money its citizens have ever enjoyed.

It was Lincoln who stated;

Money is the creature of law, and the creation of the original issue of money should be maintained as an exclusive monopoly of the National Government . . . The privilege of creating and issuing money is not only the supreme prerogative of the Government, it is the Government's greatest opportunity.

He took positive steps to fulfill his conviction.

During the early years of the Civil War, Lincoln through the Congress succeeded in issuing $450,000,000 of United States legal tender notes without one cent either of indebtedness or of interest incurred by the nation. Such constitutional money was called "greenbacks" and was secured by the assets of the entire United States. Why need a great and sovereign nation turn its credit over to private bankers to be rented back in the form of interest-bearing indebtedness? Couldn't all of the nation's money supply, geared to its economic need, be brought into existence without saddling the nation, or its people, with liabilities for the use of its own credit and assets? The answer is emphatically affirmative, but the private usurers and bondsmen had no disposition to tolerate a circumvention of their merry game of siphoning off the wealth of the nation.

There is ample evidence leading one to believe that Lincoln signed his own death warrant when he took the first bold step to abolish financial servitude. Whereas his Emancipation Proclamation decreed the abolition of physical slavery for a large segment of the population, his issuance of "green backs" decreed the abolition of economic slavery for every man, woman and child in the nation. But ruthless and avaricious financiers were not to be thwarted in their systematic sacking of the virgin territory and untapped resources of America.

Not able to stop the issuance of nearly half a billion dollars in constitutional and sound money, the banking syndicate was successful in placing a limitation on the "greenbacks" themselves. Thus these notes bore upon their face the following; "This note is a legal tender at its face value for all debts, public and private, **except duties on imports and interest on the public debt.**" It was this exception clause which forced government and importers to kowtow to private bankers and ultimately depreciated the "greenbacks." In 1879, after all the depreciated greenbacks had been bought up by financial speculators, Congress was induced to pass a law that all the notes issued during the Civil War were to be redeemed at face value in gold. It was another triumph for the nation's debt-merchants.

Lincoln's efforts not only to unmask but to destroy the Gargantuan deceit of private banking was to no avail. Nevertheless, he had made a valorous attempt to erase both over-burdening debt and pyramiding interest from the economic lives of all the generations to follow. He recognized that debt and interest are cancerous growths which devalue human toil, stiffly progress and have no place in an equitable and unfettered economy. If Lincoln had been successful in introducing the nation to a sound and honest money supply, the other built-in evils of predatory capitalism would have crumbled. One hundred years of wholesale foreclosures, hardships, anguish and periodic economic breakdowns would have been precluded.

But such was not the pattern slated for America.

In 1863 the financial barons and usurers moved with a vengeance. Holding over $2,600,000,000 of interest-bearing government bonds, which the government had been forced to sell to the banks to underwriter the costs of the Civil War, the bankers compelled the passage of the National Bank Act. The Congress was helpless to offer any opposition. Under the newly enacted law, the national banks were granted the privilege of depositing their purchased bonds with the Treasurer of the United States and then to issue up to 90% of those bonds in bank notes to private borrowers. Thus on precisely the same money they collected 6% interest on the bonds themselves and a similar interest, usually more, on the private bank notes they "manufactured."

From the time of the Civil War up to the present there is a perpetual history of how private bankers and their syndicates have inveigled out of Congress privileged and unconstitutional legislation giving them despotic control the nation's money supply. No small part of their intrigue involved their garnering of the gold and getting Congressional sanction that any money issued by the government must be redeemed in the precious metal owned by the private banks. Thus they could prevent the United States government from interfering with the bankers' exclusive monopoly.

"Mystic" Quality of Gold

Throughout the monetary history of this nation the private banks have promoted the calculated deception that gold is the only sound basis for a nation's money supply. The fact that such basis permitted them to control the money supply simply by cornering the gold supply was carefully kept from the people. What should have registered with the people with shocking impact is this challenging question: If the whole purpose of a money supply is to facilitate the exchange of goods and services, and to provide for productive expansion, why then shouldn't all money be related directly to those goods, services and production?

What twisted reasoning dictates that a nation's progress and well-being should be dependent on some mystic quality of a metal instead of being directly dependent on the natural resources, manpower and ingenuity of the whole nation and its people?

Not having any understanding of how his money was created, or more importantly, how the amount of money was arbitrarily determined, the average citizen has unsuspectingly accepted the promoted fiction that both his cash and checks were backed by gold. While it is true that prior to 1934 the legal promise existed to convert both currency and bank deposits into gold, no such amount of gold has actually existed.

For example, when the Federal Reserve was organized in 1914, the total deposits and currency in circulation amounted to 20 billion dollars, but there was only 1.6 billion dollars of monetary gold in the country. In other words, the amount of money in circulation was 12 times the amount of gold. According to figures from the House Committee on Banking and Currency, a similar proportion held true fifty years later in 1963. At that time the money supply, both cash and checks, totaled 157.4 billion dollars and the Treasury's gold was only 15.6 billion dollars.

However, citing these figures is begging the point. In 1934, the private banking institutions succeeded in pushing through a law that not only made it illegal to possess gold but no American citizen could demand gold in exchange for his dollars. As usual, of course, there was an exemption for the non-American. Foreigners holding American credit could through their banks demand, and have their dollars converted into, gold bullion.

From a private banking system based on useless bags of gold, we have come supinely to accept an entire money supply based on debt. Not one person in a thousand, more likely, not one in a hundred thousand, recognizes the hoax that private bankers have perpetrated on the nation, its citizens and its government. Unsuspectingly, the people and their government have turned over their property and their earning capacity to the private banks to be monetized and lent back to them in the form of interest-bearing indebtedness.

Slowly but surely more and more people are beginning to recognize the fallacious gimmick of fractional-reserve lending which permits the private banks to grant loans—and bear in mind that it is the people's credit that makes the loans good—five times or more the assets or reserves of the bank itself. All such granting of loans, or credit-dollars, is nothing but the **manufacture** of money. Every time a loan is made, this is money that had no existence prior to its creation by the private bank.

The arbitrary power to expand and contract the money supply, by the making of loans or calling them in, has placed in the hands of the private bankers the unhallowed power not only to change the purchasing worth of the dollar but has given them the power literally to control the amount of work the nation can perform.

The nation's entire working capacity has been made beholden to the whim and greed of those who are **non-producers**.

Inflation and Deflation

The average American has little or no understanding of the causes either of inflation or deflation of his nation's money and credit. The fundamental causes of the erosion of the dollar entirely escapes him because he has been purposely kept ignorant of how his nation's debt-money functions.

The purpose now is to cast some light on the twin mysteries of inflation and deflation, and to demonstrate how the real culprit of destroyed purchasing power is the whole privately owned and controlled banking system. For, if a person doesn't grasp the mechanics of how and why our money supply is systematically manipulated, there can be no understanding of how billions of dollars in interest, foreclosed property and savings are ruthlessly or callously wrested from the people by private debt-merchants.

The fact to be recognized is that coins and all currency constitute less than ten percent of the money supply. Over ninety percent of all the nation's monetary needs are provided for by credit in the form of loans which create demand deposits or checking accounts. It comes as a total surprise to most Americans to learn that private banks do not loan to borrowers other peoples' savings or the assets of the bank itself. Every credit-dollar that a commercial bank puts into circulation in the form of loans is **new** money that has been created.

At any given moment, the purchasing power of the people is the amount of cash and checking accounts in existence. In short, the law of supply and demand applies explicitly to the purchasing value of the unit "dollar." Increase the number of dollars in circulation and there exist high prices and a **cheap** dollar. Decrease the number of dollars in circulation and there exist low prices and a **high** dollar.

It is the manipulation by first creating a cheap dollar, with all its attendant ramifications of easy borrowing and increased indebtedness, and then creating a high dollar, with all its attendant ramifications of foreclosures and destroyed purchasing power—coupled with "administered" prices—that has resulted in every major depression and panic the nation has known since its inception. The toll paid by the American people throughout their history in hardship, suffering and heartache is immeasurable in the wake of such financial intrigue.

Startling as it may seem to most Americans, it is impossible, under our present private money system, to have prosperity, with full employment and full production, without a commensurate increase in indebtedness. It is impossible to get a single dollar of the very life-blood of our economic system into circulation without an individual, or a corporation, or the government going into debt. And for the privilege of going into debt, each must pay a tribute to the private shylocks in the form of exorbitant interest!

At this point, it should be easy to observe that when the private banking system commences to expand the money supply, making loans easy to get, we have the condition of **inflation**, a lot of new credit dollars in circulation, against which there are no existing goods and services. Immediately there is a resurgence of business. Production is increased and the unemployed go to work. New businesses are commenced to produce new items, and general prosperity and good times are at hand.

Parenthetically, however, we should note that the expansion of the money supply has not added one iota to the nation's resources, has not added one additional human being to the work force, or added one scintilla to the nation's technological know-how. Momentarily, private banking has performed no other gesture than to release its stranglehold on the nation's ability to produce. However, the "magnanimity" of its gesture is but prelude to the big steal in the making.

At the point when the nation and its people are saddled with as much indebtedness as "the traffic will bear," the private banks reverse their whole monetary policy. They commence to call in their loans and to restrict all spending. In other words, they bring about a condition of **deflation**. A circumstance has now been deliberately created in which the cash and credit in circulation is less than the goods and services that are available for purchase. Inventories become stagnant, men are thrown out of work, and the whole nation has landed in a disastrous depression.

Witness now what has really happened to the people and their government. It is only a small part of the tragic picture to point out the slowdown of the economy, the hunger, the millions unemployed. The real crime of private banking is that while the people and their government incurred their indebtedness during a period of inflation when a dollar was cheap, they have now to pay off their debts with a dollar that is high. **Human effort throughout the whole spectrum of the economy has been devalued.**

This is the harvest time for the private banks and lending institutions. Not only is there unavoidable wholesale foreclosure on homes, farms and small businesses, but every dollar of both public and private indebtedness must be paid back by future earnings made up of a dollar representing increased human effort. Hundreds of billions of dollars are added to the coffers of the unscrupulous financiers by thus inflating and deflating the nation's money supply. It is a high price that the people must pay to enjoy only a temporary prosperity. It is the inevitable consequence of a money system that is based on debt.

Vampiristic Interest

The power to inflate and deflate the money supply by arbitrarily creating debt-dollars is only half the picture. Equally devastating to the economy, and thus affecting the lives of all the people, is the whole spectrum of ruinous interest. Every credit dollar that is put into circulation by the private commercial banks is in the form of interest-bearing indebtedness.

In a few paragraphs it would be impossible to cover adequately this evil which has plagued mankind up the centuries, an evil that all major religions in their earliest histories both denounced and forbade. However, we should have a minimal grasp of the pyramiding effect of interest in order to understand the impact it has on our fortunes, our lives, and the stranglehold it currently exerts in suffocating the whole economy.

We can get some idea of the billions of dollars, the hundreds of billions, paid in interest solely on the public debt by considering President Lincoln's issuance of "green backs" which were the only "money" this nation has ever had without incurring debt or interest. If that $450,000,000, less than one-half billion dollars, had been put into circulation by turning over to the private banks interest-bearing bonds, the accumulated interest today, according to computations by the Treasury Department, would be over 40 billion dollars.

Now give thought to a whole monetary history of the Federal government beholden to private usurers for use of the nation's own credit. The magnitude of the interest charges on the Federal debt should be apparent. From a Federal debt of less than one billion dollars in 1800, the debt has risen to the current over-burdening amount of over 360 billion dollars. It is a whole history of indebtedness with a sovereign people naively paying the private bankers hundreds of billions of dollars for use of the people's own credit.

Today the interest on the Federal debt alone is 16 billion dollars, second only to national defense as the largest item in the national budget. If during the next 24 years there is no increase in indebtedness; the accumulated interest on the Federal debt will exceed the total amount of the principal, with the 360 billion dollars in debt still burdening the nation and the people.

To get a glimpse into the astronomical amounts that the private banks extort out of the economy is to consider two very simple facts. The first is that any amount of money loaned at 6% compound-interest doubles itself every 12years. The second fact is that of geometric progression, where if one takes a mere penny and doubles it, and then doubles each total for thirty times, one will come up with the incredible grand total of over

5 million dollars. It is the foregoing two facts, plus the fact that the vast bulk of loans by the private banks are simply book entries and are not made up of the deposits of others or assets of the bank itself, that makes interest-taking so insidious, so pernicious, and so astronomical.

Perhaps we can get a sufficient appreciation of unmitigated exploitation that is reflected in exorbitant interest charges by considering a statistical table placed in the. Congressional Record by Representative Wright Patman on July 27, 1967. This table covers the interest paid on both the public and private debt for each year from 1951 to 1966. The significance of the 15-year table is that it compares what the interest would have been if interest rates had been kept at the 1951 level.

In 1951, the total indebtedness, private and public, was 524 billion dollars. In 1966, the total indebtedness, private and public, had pyramided to 1,368.3 billion dollars—over one and a third trillion dollars. During this 15-year period, the American people and their government have paid in interest the staggering sum of 680.2 billion dollars. If the interest rates had not been unnecessarily increased, the total interest paid would have been 468.5 billion dollars.

The net result is that from 1951 to 1966 the private banking system, through the interest manipulation of the banker-dominated Federal Reserve, extorted $211,700,000,000 (211.7 **billion** dollars) from the citizenry.

Representative Patman, in presenting these official statistics, stated,

> These figures plainly establish that high interest rates have been a burdensome tax on the low and moderate income families. High interest rates have deprived these people of huge chunks of their wages and at the same time have prevented the construction of needed housing and other works.

He further commented:

> The Federal Reserve has acted as destructively as the worst of the rioters. And the resulting damage to the economy has far exceeded the damage from all the riots. The Federal Reserve's December 6, 1965 defiance of the President wiped out the chance to build 500,000 new housing units in 1966—for more than have been burned or destroyed in all the riots combined.

To appreciate the magnitude of the excessive interest paid only in the year 1966 is to make a comparison with farm income. In so doing we should realize that there are approximately 3.4 million farms, and that these millions of farms are responsible for supplying the food that nourishes all our citizens. In addition, these millions of farms provide much of the fibre used in making the nation's clothing. Now consider the fact that the excessive interest paid only in the year 1966, which was 36 billion dollars, was the same amount as the total gross farm receipts from marketings in 1963. Incredible as it might seem, the **excessive interest** of non-producers in one year was equal to the **total output** of the nation's producers who sustain life for 200,000,000 citizens!

Let's give some thought to the total of 211.7 billion dollars that represents the excessive interest for the past fifteen years. A hypothetical construction project of building houses priced at $20,000 per unit would seem to give us a good yardstick. As we construct each 50-foot house, we butt each next to the other with no space between. For 211 billion dollars, how long a line of houses would we have constructed? We would have constructed a line of houses, each butted against the next, going around the world four times.

While interest charges are involved in everything that is purchased, in no area is its evil more apparent than in home buying. However, in too few cases, particularly the young couple desperate to get a home of their own, are the buyers aware that they are the victims of a merciless game of paying double the amount in human effort for value received. Month in and month out, during the best years of their lives, the nation's homeowners are paying for two houses but receiving only one. In fact, the average couple is unaware that, because of exorbitant interest charges, their home is depreciating faster than they are able to reduce the mortgage.

Certainly, it should dawn on the nation's homeowners, or home-builders, that they not only give a first mortgage on their home to the bank but that it is their earning capacity that makes the loan substantive. In short, the average home-builder must pay the voracious money-lender in interest an amount equal to the price of the home for the use of the home-builder's own credit while the moneylender doesn't as much as replace one shingle or plant one seed of grass during a 25-year period of receiving payments.

There are no economic crimes against humanity comparable to the diabolical power to manufacture a nation's money and to charge tributes called interest. A halt must be called to the whole business. The same element that makes the citizen's mortgage and the government's bond good for the private banker is the same element that would allow sovereign people the right to provide for their own monetary needs without either the burden of debt or interest.

Federal Reserve System

In 1913 the Federal Reserve Act was passed. Under the guise of setting up a flexible money system that would meet the commercial and individual credit needs of an expanding economy, the private bankers pushed through Congress a system of money control that gave them despotic power in determining the whole money supply of the nation. Consequently, up here in the 1960's, a mere handful of men, occupying the highest positions in the private banking complex, exercise a life-

and-death influence over the lives of every man, exceeding the combined power of both the President and the entire Congress.

The key to an understanding of how the Federal Reserve System is a private-banker-oriented and dominated autocracy is the fact that of the nine directors of each of the 12 Federal Reserve Banks, six are elected by the private member banks. A questionnaire sent out in 1964 by the House Banking and Currency Committee revealed that even of the 36 directors elected by the Federal Reserve Board, 19 were, or had been, connected with the private banking industry. In short, 91 out of the total 108 directors of the Federal Reserve Banks had connections or associations with the private banks which they were supposed to regulate.

The arrogant statement of William McChesney Martin before the Joint Economic Committee of the U. S. Congress on February 26, 1965, should leave little doubt as to the fact that it is the wishes of the private bankers that the Board serves and not the people whose earnings and savings should be protected. Testifying before the Committee, Chairman Martin brazenly stated that "the Federal Reserve Board has the authority to act independently of the President," even "despite the President." Ten months later, the Federal Reserve Board demonstrated its sell-proclaimed autocracy by arbitrarily raising the interest rate despite the pleadings of President Johnson to the contrary.

Open Market Committee

However, not the Federal Reserve Board, nor the Federal Reserve Banks, are the real power over the nation's money. The fundamental and dictatorial monetary powers of the nation are exercised by a committee that most Americans do not know even exists. This is the Open Market Committee which is made up technically of five Federal Reserve Bank presidents and the seven members of the Federal Reserve Board. However, all twelve presidents of the Federal Reserve Banks participate in its deliberations.

The Open Market Committee is not only the most powerful single group of men in this nation, but perhaps in the world. Meeting in secret, immune from public auditing or disclosure of the minutes of its meetings, its operations of buying and selling government securities give it absolute and autocratic control over the nation's entire money supply. In the hands of this Committee exists the power to inflate or deflate arbitrarily the amount of money to conduct the over-all economy. Through its actions literally billions of dollars in interest and foreclosures flow into the private bankers' coffers while at the same time the nation needlessly suffers economic breakdown, unemployment, business stagnation and spiraling indebtedness.

There was no provision for the Open Market Committee in the Federal Reserve Act of 1913. The intent of the Act was to set up twelve semiautonomous Federal Banks that would provide the necessary reserves for its members by monetizing the "eligible" short-term commercial paper, thereby responding to business conditions and requirements of each regional area of the nation. The Federal Reserve Board would determine the discount rates and interest rates, thus serving as a check on the amount of reserves the commercial banks would have against which to make loans.

In less than ten years after the enactment of the Act, the powerful private banks in the East had succeeded in thwarting the specific intent of the Federal Reserve System by converting it into a central banking system by the setting up of an **ad hoc** committee to coordinate the buying and selling of government bonds. Later they succeeded in pressuring Congress to give legality to the Open Market Committee which gave the private banks absolute control over the nation's money supply.

Today it has a portfolio of over 40 billion dollars in government bonds which have been paid for once by the taxpayers with Federal Reserve notes and therefore should be retired. Instead these billions of dollars in government securities continue to collect interest and are the primary source of "reserves" for the commercial banks for placing the nation further and further in debt.

Bankers Testify Under Oath

To those who are unacquainted with the ramifications of money control, it may be a surprise to learn that shelf upon shelf of books have been written upon the subject. The incredible circumstance is that so much knowledge could exist without sufficient people rising in enlightened protest to demand monetary reform. (See the bibliography for a partial listing of the best books on the subject.

While there has been no dearth of information available on either the forces or personalities behind money control or the diabolical power that they have exercised, and do exercise, the real difficulty has been in getting large enough numbers of people to accept the truth of the allegations.

One of the chief obstacles has been that most of the writings on, and analyses of, money and banking have embodied very little direct testimony by bankers themselves. Thus the accused could continue to promote the doubt in the reader's mind that the accusers were presenting an erroneous case. Like the yokel who saw a giraffe for the first time, the reader was conditioned to react, "There just ain't such an animal!"

Of very recent time, a most fortunate development came to pass. It was to work the end of any deceptive counteraction that those who were endeavoring to awaken the people to the iniquitous machinations of private banking were subverters of the public trust and advocates of "funny-money" schemes. Out of the mouths of bankers themselves, under oath, was to come the whole story of the workings of their own nefarious system.

For the whole year of 1964, spring, and fall, a committee of the United States Congress conducted extensive hearings into the operations of the Federal Reserve system. No aspect or ramification of the 50-year existence of the nation's banking system was left unscrutinized. It was the first time in the history of the nation that a duly constituted Committee of Congress had so penetratingly and thoroughly investigated the issuance and control of our whole money supply.

The man who spearheaded the investigation was Representative Wright Patman of Texas who is the Chairman of the House Committee on Banking and Currency, and was also chairman of the Subcommittee on House Finance which was responsible for the hearings. It should be noted that Rep. Patman has been for 40 years one of the nation's most knowledgeable and forceful critics of the privately controlled Federal Reserve System. He has stressed consistently that under the Constitution it is the right and duty of Congress to create and control the money supply and that under the Federal Reserve Act passed on December 13, 1913, and subsequent Acts, the absolute power over the nation's money has been exercised by private bankers.

The hearings are too voluminous for the average person to read en toto. However, for the scholar there is now available an historic and documented record of how private banking operates and how the nation's whole economy is despotically influenced by its actions. Not only were all the executives of the Federal Reserve System itself, the 12 presidents of the Federal Reserve Banks and the seven members of the Federal Reserve Board, meticulously interrogated but included as well were the Secretary of the Treasury, officials of the General Accounting Office, representatives of the American Bankers Association, the Independent Bankers Association and representatives of the commercial banks.

Included also were dozens of experts representing a wide range of testimony. Among them were the President of the Cooperative League, the research director of the AFL-CIO, past advisors to Presidents Truman and Kennedy, and a number of outstanding authorities on law, political economy and public administration. In addition, many statements and exhibits were all made part of the hearings. The three volumes entitled "The Federal Reserve System After Fifty Years" which cover the hearings fill over 2200 pages alone. Corollary volumes make a stack of priceless documentation over a foot high.

At the conclusion of the hearings the majority of members of the Subcommittee made specific recommendations, and later introduced bills, for the express purpose of reversing high interest rates and tight money, and curbing the exorbitant power of the private banks which control the Federal Reserve System. At this writing all such effort has been smothered by the pressure and intimidation of the financial lobbies spearheaded by the American Bankers Association. Under no circumstances do they intend to tolerate legislative interference with their monopolistic control of the nation's credit and money supply.

The extent to which the banking lobbies will go is graphically borne out by the attempted bribe of Representative Gonzales, a member of the Subcommittee from Texas. Representative Gonzales testified that he had been offered a position on the Board of Directors of a bank coupled with a stock gift amounting to $14,000. One can only speculate as to how many elected representatives, over the years, have succumbed to overtures of barefaced bribery.

Summary

Throughout the history of this nation private banking has been the exploitive and lucrative business of the privileged few to put **unearned** claims, or purchasing power, into circulation to compete with the **earned** claims of all who work, produce and perform services. It is the incredible process by which every dollar that is put into circulation is in the form of interest-bearing indebtedness. The individual must give the bank his mortgage. His government must give the bank its bonds. The banks give no **equivalent value** in return.

Surely, it behooves every American to understand how private control of money functions and how he and his fellow citizens have been victimized. When he realizes the full scope of the "crimes" which can be charged to private banking, he will be moved, at least figuratively, to disintegrate the whole financial colossus with his own bare hands. The legalized crimes of private control of a nation's money supply cover more than the hundreds of billions of dollars extorted from the people in usury, and the much, much greater amounts represented in the homes, farms and businesses wrested from the people by foreclosure.

They cover as well the whole area of what the people **might** have enjoyed, and how the nation could have progressed, if there had existed an honest and adequate monetary system.

The power to control the nation's money supply is the power to determine the value, or purchasing power, of every dollar earned and every dollar spent. But it is more. It is the power to determine the people's ability to buy homes, to acquire the necessities of life, to educate their children, to pay their bills, and to remit their taxes. It is the power to determine the degree of survival and well-being of all the people.

Control of a nation's money supply is the most powerful monopoly any group can exercise, leading to the impoverishing, the bondaging and the subjugating of a whole citizenry. Such control and exercise has been tragically the monetary history of America.

Viewing our history in retrospect, it taxes the imagination to realize that a young and fertile land, filled with such an energetic and ingenious people, should have been betrayed so long to the connivings of those who were non-producers. How utterly incredible that debt-merchants, with nothing but their garnered bags of gold, and their usurped power to create interest-bearing debt, could so long systematically bilk a nation without an outraged citizenry making them disgorge their unearned wealth and unearned claims!

The answer lies of course in a number of circumstances which we have alluded to earlier. Overridingly, it has been the circumstance of the majority of the people caught in the throes of eking out an existence being too preoccupied to enlighten themselves about the subject of money. Others recognized that to protest was to jeopardize their economic livelihood, besides having the stigma attached to their person that they were advocates of "funny money." There has always been a penalty for being too brash in indicting the pernicious power of private banking.

When we come to consider the basic economic renovations and reform that the nation must embrace, we will specifically deal with "money" and the true role it should play in a constructive economy. You will see the idiocy of turning its issuance and control over to those whose greed and lust for power blinds them to the human needs of a nation.

The American people must come to recognize that banking must be solely a function of the people's government. Secondly, the credit of the United States is sufficient in itself to back all the nation's monetary needs without incurring one cent of indebtedness. Thirdly, the purchasing value of the totality of money must be equal to the totality of goods and services which are purchasable. In the fourth place, "money" must come into existence automatically as the sovereign people utilize their maximum productive potential for achieving the maximum good life for each and every citizen.

This would be an honest and adequate money supply insuring freedom and prosperity.

Chapter 16

ARTIFICIAL ENTITIES VS. HUMAN BEINGS

MOST Americans, from schoolchild to adult, subscribe to the idealism that America is a nation founded four-square on individual liberty. Not only was the nation born by winning its liberation from foreign tyranny, but the document signifying American independence underscores in ringing words the **inalienable** rights of every human being to "life, liberty and the pursuit of happiness."

The Preamble to the Constitution is equally adamant in emphasizing the paramount importance of the people by stating, "We, **the people** of the United States, in order to . . . secure the blessings of liberty to **ourselves** and our **posterity**, do ordain and establish this Constitution for the United States of America."

Unequivocally, the intent of those who founded this nation was to make the people supreme both as the shapers of their own destiny and as the prime beneficiaries of the nation's full potential. This was the America envisioned by our forebears. It was people, as human beings, who were to be protected, enlightened, enhanced and each given equal opportunity to develop his full inborn capabilities. Everything else was to be subordinate to human beings. Property, institutions, and government itself, were to be the tools and servants of man in his constant search to achieve his own betterment.

This is the America that most Americans still think they live in, although the disillusioned grow to greater and greater numbers. Knowledgeable citizens are aware that this idealistic America just does not exist and has not existed during the larger part of the nation's history. They are aware that behind all the paeans to liberty and the stereotyped Fourth of July oratory quite a different America came into being and is, at the present time, dominant. From a nation formed and predicated on the **divine rights of man** was to emerge progressively a nation shaped, controlled and dominated by the "divine rights" of **property and power**.

Since the founding of the nation, two Americas have existed. They can be identified as the America of human entities and the America of artificial entities. The history of the nation has been a constant struggle between these two forces in our society. It has been an incessant battle between **natural** persons seeking expression of "life, liberty and the pursuit of happiness" and the growth and power of **unnatural** persons—corporate monopolies—whose very success was directly dependent on thwarting or destroying the individual's well-being and self-reliance.

Certainly the men who founded this nation, those who championed the inherent rights of man, never envisioned an ultimate condition in. America in which a mere couple of hundred multi-billion-dollar corporate giants would be oppressively dominant in the entire economy of the nation. There is no evidence that the Founding Fathers ever meant that the natural rights of human beings should be emasculated and negated by financial, industrial and political oligarchies. This, however, does not mean that they did not have serious misgivings about the sovereign citizens being able to protect their natural rights against institutions and corporations accumulating increased property and wielding abnormal power.

James Madison, esteemed as the Father of the Constitution, on August 7, 1787 in the Constitutional Convention, warned as follows:

> In future times a great majority of the people will not only be without land, but any other sort of property. These will either combine under the influence of their common situation, in which case the rights of property and the public liberty will not be secure in their hands

or, which is more probable, they will become the tools of opulence and ambition, in which case there will be equal danger on another side.

Later that same year, Thomas Jefferson, in a letter to James Madison, on December 20, 1787, clearly voiced his misgivings in regard to the economic inadequacy of the Constitution then pending ratification by listing among his objections:

First, the omission of a bill of rights, providing dearly, and without the aid of sophism, for . . . restriction of monopolies.

There were other misgivings and warnings and fears expressed by other framers of the Constitution concerning monopolies, including some from States reluctant to ratify. However, in light of the abundance of land for a predominantly agricultural economy, and being concerned primarily with the task of instituting popular government, the Founding Fathers placed their reliance in oncoming generations to protect their economic rights. Perhaps they innocently felt that Constitutional guarantees, particularly the Fifth Amendment, would afford future citizens sufficient protection against ever being deprived of that which rightfully belonged to them.

Viewing our history in retrospect, we Americans of the Twentieth Century might well stand aghast at the extent to which the entire nation was left easy prey for the avaricious, the ambitious and the unscrupulous. Only the vast natural wealth of the country and the indefatigable industry of its people have served to offset the depredations of those determined to exploit and control. But even these factors were inadequate to check the ultimate ascendancy of artificial entities to absolute economic power over the entire citizenry.

One chapter could not even attempt to portray the chronological and systematic pillaging of this nation by artificial entities in the form of corporations, trusts, holding companies and a myriad investment and speculative combines. At the end of this volume is a bibliography which contains documented books covering not only the whole gamut of robber barons who through their corporate entities sacked the natural wealth of this nation long before the turn of the present century, but covering also the industrial cartels of this Twentieth Century which have corralled ownership and control of the real wealth of the nation up here in the latter half of the 1960's.

Concentration of Wealth Throughout History

Americans who naively assume that this nation has existed and functioned for the benefit of human beings, and none other, are in for a real jolt when they acquaint themselves with the documented story of the pyramided fortunes of the Astors, the Fields, the Vanderbilts, the Goulds, the Morgans, the Schiffs, the Mellons, the Warburgs, the Rockefellers and the artificial entities they set up to accumulate their fantastic fortunes. From the earliest shipping companies, up through all the machinations in railroading, oil, ores, industry and banking, right up to the present time, it is a story of fraud, swindles, privileged legislation, and a depriving of the people and their government of both the fruits of their efforts and their rightful assets.

The growth and power of corporate interests have been in direct ratio to the deprivation of the ordinary people. While artificial entities waxed affluent and powerful, there has always been the parallel tragedy of the preponderant number of people enduring successive panics, being caught in the throes of foreclosure and unemployment, and always being forced to put liens against their future earnings in order to keep body and soul together.

Too many Americans, who are even to some degree aware of the current concentration of the nation's producing assets, think of the past history of the nation as one of equal distribution of wealth. They are unaware that before the turn of this current

154

century, the real wealth had all been garnered by the few. According to the census of 1890, a mere nine percent of the entire population owned **seventy-one percent** of all wealth. As for the majority, up fifty-two percent of the population, they owned but **five percent** of all property, land and assets.

The trend toward greater and greater concentration continued. In 1915, the Report of the Industrial Commission revealed that of the total wealth of 140 billion dollars, the top two percent of the population owned 60% ($84 billion), the middle 33 % percent owned 35 % ($49 billion), and the poor, constituting 65% of the entire population, owned but 5% or a mere $7 billion.

Since World War I, which witnessed an impetus to corporate growth, up to the present time there is an inescapable, documented picture of the corporate take-over of this nation. It is a picture of the little farmer, the little manufacturer and the little retailer being either forced out of business or being swallowed up by monopolistic enterprises. It is a picture of the tens of millions, the vast majority, as workers, consumers and taxpayers underwriting the development of the nation's whole economic capacity without receiving any equity in the tangible assets they made possible. It is a picture of tens of millions enduring enforced poverty and a nation becoming increasingly burdened with spiraling indebtedness.

One can become fuzzy-eyed reading the statistics that are now available in documented books and Congressional investigating committees, particularly the committees on anti-trust and monopoly, which substantiate overwhelmingly the concentrated ownership of the nation's real wealth. No longer is there any dearth of evidence as to the despotic ownership that exists in every field of economic endeavor. In manufacturing, in merchandising, in transportation, in communication, in insurance, in banking and in farming there exists an across-the-board picture of a small minority of the population owning and directing the oligarchic corporate entities which in turn control the nation's entire economic life.

In the Congressional Record of February 17, 1969, Senator Philip A. Hart, Chairman of the Subcommittee on Antitrust and Monopoly stated:

> Our Subcommittee has developed figures which I think cannot be refuted, showing that about twothirds of American industrial capacity and output currently is in the hands of 200—200 corporations, they call them, but 200 management decisions that affect two-thirds of our output—and the trend rapidly accelerates.

Administered Prices in 90% of All Industry

No dispassionate researcher can read the many volumes of hearings that make up the investigations of the Senate Subcommittee on Antitrust and Monopoly, first under the chairmanship of the late Senator Estes Kefauver during the 1950's and the early 1960's and since under Senator Hart, without recognizing not only the take-over of the economy by a couple of hundred corporate giants but also recognizing that the classical marketplace exists only as a promoted myth. In the volume "Economic Concentration-Part 1, Overall and Conglomerate Aspects, 1964" on page 253 and 254, Mr. Chumbris, one of the chief counsels for the Subcommittee made these pertinent conclusions:

> ... for the last 7 years, pretty much under the direction of Dr. Blair (chief economist for the Subcommittee) this subcommittee has been trying to show that we are not in system in this country where the classical marketplace competition is determined, but everything is determined by administered prices.
>
> I think we started with hearings on July 8 of 1957, to be exact, with Dr. Means, Dr. Galbraith and three or four other economists, some of whom came here and told us

that there is no such thing as the classical marketplace competition today. If we take the theory of administered prices they said, 90 percent of everything we do in business today is under administered prices, and Dr. Means and a few other economists have testified that it would be wonderful to go back to the old classical theory as he called it of competition, but that is not the way we can do business today. How can the subcommittee for 7 years say there is no such thing as a marketplace that determines classical competition but we have administered price theory in this country, where 90 percent of our industry is controlled by administered prices, and then say that we are going to go back to what you call the classical competitive theory?

Ninety percent of all industry controlled by administered prices! Which is just another way of saying that monopolies controlled 90 percent of all industry and exercised the usurped power "to tax" through price-fixing.

This was in 1964 and since that time the whole rash of mergers, conglomerates and one-bank holding companies has further concentrated the economic power along with further destruction of so called "competition" in the open marketplace.

"Top of the Top"

Most people giving any serious thought to the concentration of economic power in the nation are familiar with **Fortune's** annual listing of the nation's 500 largest industrials, the 50 largest commercial banks, the 50 largest life insurance companies, the 50 largest retailers, the 50 largest transportation companies and the 50 largest utilities. These 750 corporate giants exceed in assets and scope of operation the remaining over 10,000,000 enterprises that make up the nation's entire economy. In fact, as graphically portrayed in "The Limits of American Capitalism" by Robert Heilbroner, to remove a mere 150 of the largest of these corporations from the economy would mean the complete collapse of the economic structure.

However, the concentration of assets and economic power is reflected in a considerably smaller number of corporations which are the super-corporations of the nation's economy.

Let us first direct our attention to the **Fortune** magazine of June 15, 1968. Under the title, "The Top of the Top", are listed the thirty-eight largest corporations in the nation. To qualify in this list a corporation must have assets of at least **4 billion** dollars. It is pertinent to note that in the previous year there were only 31 companies that qualified, thus seven new companies had risen in assets to be numbered with those occupying the very top seats of power in super-capitalism.

We now come in for an astounding revelation. The total assets of these super-giant corporations come to over **363 billion dollars**. Incredible as it must seem to those who still think of this nation as one of small shops and small businesses, these 38 corporations have assets which are more than the **combined** assets of the 500 largest industrial corporations, and almost equal to the total assets of 712 corporations making up the balance of the 750 corporations listed by **Fortune.**

What type of corporations make up this "Top of the Top" listing of 38 super giants? To the uniformed it is surprising to learn that fourteen are banks and nine are life insurance companies. In checking the list as to rank, one finds that after the No.1, American Telephone and Telegraph, with assets approaching 38 billion dollars, comes Prudential Insurance with 25 billion, Metropolitan Life Insurance with 24 billion, Bank: of America with 21 billion, Chase Manhattan Bank: with nearly 18 billion, and then First National City Bank with 17 billion. Then after Standard Oil (New Jersey) and General Motors come 6 more banks and insurance companies before reaching Ford Motor Co. and Texaco on the list.

One-bank Holding Companies

The significance of the rank of the private banks in the list of the super-corporations is noteworthy in light of the current, audacious moves by the nation's largest banks in setting up one-bank holding companies in order to create financial-industrial conglomerates. Before we give thought to this new trend of the private banks opening combining with industry, we should recognize that just as a handful of super-corporations have a monopoly in industry and services, so do a mere handful of super-banks have a monopoly in private banking.

In a public release, on December 10, 1965, Representative Wright Patman, chairman of the House Committee on Banking and Currency, had this to say:

> We are already far down the road to monopoly and concentration in banking. Today 100 out of 14,000 banks—less than 1 percent—control 50 percent of the nation's banking assets. 14 big banks have 25 percent of the deposits.

Evidence of even greater concentration was given by Representative Patman speaking on the NBC "Today" show on July 10, 1969, when he stated that out of the nation's 13,000 banks, 24 banks controlled over 50% of banking assets.

No one should have any difficulty in recognizing that the linkup of the nation's largest banks with the nation's largest industrial corporations marks the final takeover by the minority that dominates under private capitalism. The economic handwriting is clear. When 100 banks which control over 50 percent of the nation's banking assets and less than 100 corporations which own over two-thirds of the nation's producing assets combine, it is inevitable that a few dozen super-super conglomerates will soon own and direct the nation's entire resources and producing machinery.

Certainly the foregoing projection is more than speculation when someone like Secretary of the Treasury Kennedy, himself a past associate of the super-banks, expresses alarm. In the **Fortune** magazine for May 15, 1969, the Secretary of the Treasury projected what is in store for America in view of the current acceleration of setting up one-bank holding companies. His projection was in these succinct terms:

> We would find ourselves in a structure dominated by some fifty to seventy-five huge centers of economic and financial power—each of which would consist of a corporate conglomerate controlling a large bank or a multi-billion-dollar bank controlling a large nonfinancial conglomerate.

Secretary Kennedy undoubtedly had reference to such one-bank holding companies as Chase Manhattan Corporation which was created by Chase Manhattan Bank which ranks fifth on the "Top of the Top" list of the super-corporations with the largest assets. And to such other one-bank holding companies as J.P. Morgan & Co., Inc. of which Morgan Guaranty is a subsidiary, and Conil Corporation of which Continental Illinois Bank is now a unit. It should be noted that Morgan Guaranty and Continental Illinois Bank are 12th and 22nd respectively on the list of the nation's "Top of the Top" largest corporations.

The extent of the current expansion of private banks into financial-industrial conglomerates is evidenced by the fact that more than 100 financial institutions, with nearly one-third of the nation's deposits, have formed such "congeneric" one-bank holding companies. These 100 private banks include 21 of **Fortune's** list of the 50 largest commercial banks.

More powerful than government

It is obviously no exaggeration to state that artificial entities, in terms of the multi-billion-dollar monopolistic corporations, not only exercise power greater than government itself but in reality dictate the very policy of government. A conglomerate like AT&T (American Telephone and Telegraph Company), owning assets of 38 billion dollars, had gross revenue in 1967 greater than those of the five largest State governments combined—California, New York, Texas, Pennsylvania and Michigan.

Only in a lesser degree do we find the same relation of such multi-billion-dollar industrial corporations as Standard Oil, General Motors, Ford Motors, U.S. Steel, and such multi-billion-dollar bank and insurance corporations as Bank of America and Prudential Insurance.

Perhaps the gigantic size of the top corporations is the most geographically portrayed by comparing their scope of operation to government. In so doing we are only able to place the Federal Government itself on the top before commencing to list corporations as to size of business. On a gradient scale with the Federal Government first, we must then list **eight** corporations before we get to the State of California. In turn we must list another **five** corporations before arriving at New York State and New York City. We must list **ten** more corporations before getting to the state of Pennsylvania.

When we give thought to the political control of the nation, we will recognize that it is the billion-dollar lobbies of the giant corporations that really shape the makeup of Congress and dictate the functioning of government.

The vast majority of the members of Congress get elected by the direct or indirect underwriting of the large corporations. The major political parties are but the fronts of the economic power structures with the principal political leaders of both major parties heavy stockholders.

Toleration of the Small Operator

Those not fully cognizant of the advantages enjoyed by monopolies in terms of exclusive markets, sheer volume, utilization of the most advanced technology, and privileged legislation, still naively think that the small retailer or manufacturer is a competitor. The truth is that the small businesses could be squeezed out of existence in a very short time if the monopolists desired to do so. What the average person is not aware of is that it is to the advantage of the monopolies to keep in existence a sprinkling of small operators, throughout the whole economy.

The first consideration on the part of the monopolies is that the small businesses, despite their numberings some ten millions, make negligible inroads into the over-all volume of the nation's business. With less than 200 corporations owning the majority of industrial and service assets, the plethora of small enterprises constitute no threat whatsoever to the multi-billion-dollar corporations.

The second consideration is that the mere toleration of little businesses perpetuates the economic myths of "free enterprise" and "open marketplace" and blinds the people to the harsh fact that monopolistic ownership and control exists in every field of economic endeavor.

The third consideration on the part of the monopolies is the one most important to them from a practical standpoint. It is the use of the small businesses throughout the land **to justify** the exorbitant "administered" prices of the monopolies. It should be apparent to all that if only the monopolies existed, they would be scrutinized and analysis made as to why their prices were so high. The public would have all its attention focused on the operations of the monopolies. Certainly, millions of consumers would seriously ask why they should pay prices that give a handful of stockholders all the profits of the economy and why the consumers should pay prices that include the underwriting of billions of dollars in expansion of assets in which the consumers get no equity.

"If you think our prices too high, why don't you buy from your local businessman?" is the spoken or unspoken retort of the monopolies. The monopolies are simply using the small operators, both in manufacturing and retailing, to justify the price-fixing of the monopolies. The subtlety employed to call the consumers' attention to the slightly higher prices of the small operators, using them as scapegoats, so that the nation's consumers won't give studied thought to the fact that most "administered" prices are double, triple, and often ten times, what they should be.

The ultimate of private capitalism is to leave no room for small businesses within the economic framework. Only as they serve the interests of monopolies are they tolerated.

Myth of a Stockholding Citizenry

Of course, extollers of the "glories" of the private capitalist system have persistently promoted the myth that the ordinary, common citizens are the stockholders in this nation, and through dividends receive their proportionate share of profits. These apologists fail to state that out of the twenty million stockholders in the nation a mere handful at the top own more than all the rest combined. Irrefutable documentation destroys the fiction that the American people have any appreciable ownership of the nation's monopolies.

Such documentation can now be found in such books as the recent and widely read "The Rich and the Super-Rich," by Ferdinand Lundberg, and "Monopoly," a discussion of AT&T by Joseph C. Goulden, as well as in the reports of a number university research projects and many government documents.

Two independent studies, one by Professor Robert J. Lampman of the University of Wisconsin for the National Bureau of Economic Research, and another by the Survey

Research Center of the University of Michigan, covering studies spanning 1922 to 1963, substantiate the concentrated ownership that exists both as to corporations and particularly as to their stockholders. These findings leave no doubt that we have become a nation of the fabulously rich and powerful at the top with a vast array of peasants at the bottom.

The above studies brought out that of an adult population of 103 million in 1953 less than two percent, **1.6%**, owned **32%** of all privately owned wealth in the nation. Such ownership consisted of 82.2% of all stock, 100% of state and local (tax exempt) bonds, 38.2% of mortgages and notes, 13.3% of life insurance reserves, 5.9% of pension and retirement funds, 18.2% of miscellaneous property, 16.1% of real estate and 22.1% of all debts and mortgages.

As to stockholding by the majority, the 1960 University of Michigan's "Survey of Consumer Finances" showed that of all the 54 million spending units (one or more persons established as a household) 86% owned no stock at all. Of those with incomes between $5000 and $7000, 81% owned no stock. Of those with incomes between $7,500 and $10,000, 78% owned no stock. Bearing in mind that anyone qualifies as a stockholder if he owns only one share worth 50 cents, it is indeed a sophistry to portray the general public as the ordinary and across-the-board stockholders in America's monopolistic enterprises.

Indeed, it is sheer deception when a conglomerate of wealth such as AT&T pictures a little old grandma in their ads with a caption implying she is one of their typical stockholders!

No need to dwell on 40% poverty in the nation. However, the aforementioned study brings out the revealing fact that 52% (over half of the entire population) own less than $1,800 each in total assets. This means all their possessions, their second-hand car, their worn-out furniture and the shirts on their backs.

If anyone should question the fact that we are a nation of peons amidst abundance they should devote a few hours to reading the four volumes of hearings before the Select

Committee on Nutrition and Human Needs of the United States Senate, which were held during December, 1968 and January and February of 1969.

Senator George McGovern, Chairman of the Select Committee on Nutrition and Human Needs, in pleading for urgent relief for the millions hungry in the nation had this to say on April 29, 1969 when he addressed the Senate:

> We have already seen more than enough to know that many Americans are hungry now. They have been hungry for years . . . Thousands of youngsters will continue to die at birth, many thousands more will suffer irreparable brain damage and stunted overall growth. The inescapable fact is that millions (8 million!) of our fellow citizens are caught in the grip of malnutrition now.

There is one overriding cause of hunger and malnutrition—inadequate income.

200,000 Households

There is no need to belabor statistics. However, a few additional statistics are indicated because it is the concentrated ownership of the nation's **investment assets** in the leading corporations which constitute the real economic power. We should have as clear a picture is obtained from the comprehensive study prepared for the Board of Governors of the Federal Reserve System, titled "Survey of Financial Characteristics of Consumers." The survey as of December 31, 1962.

The unadorned and unmistakable picture that presents itself is that of the then 58 million households in the nation, only 1.4 million of them owned 65% of all investments assets which as aforementioned are the basis of economic control. But exercisable control is lodged with even a much smaller group of stockholders.

In the upper echelon of the foregoing 1.4 million household are a mere 200,000 households which own 32% of all investment assets. There is realism in stating that with this small group, less than half of 1% of all the households in America, lies the real economic power in the nation. When one appreciates that as little as 5% of stock ownership is sufficient, according to experts on corporate control, to dictate the policies of a large corporation, and when one appreciates that the top stock owners are largely members of extended family groups, one can readily recognize that the 32% stock ownership of the 200,000 household is more than ample in giving them dominant control of the major monopolistic corporation.

It is most revealing to learn that 60 percent of the current ownership of all stock was obtained by inheritance.

Rugged individualism, indeed!

The "Military-industrial Complex"

There is now a clear, documented picture of the complete domination of the nation's whole economy by 150 conglomerates of wealth which are in turn majority-owned by **less than 2%** of the entire citizenry, with perhaps but one-quarter of that small ownership actually controlling and directing the nation's productive capacity. It is rather an overwhelming concentration of power when it is realized that if the top 20 monopolies in each sector of economy were suddenly to cease operating, the whole nation would come to an abrupt standstill. Complete economic collapse would be the fate of the nation.

However, to understand the foregoing concentration— underscored by the fact that 90 percent of all industry in the nation is engaged in price-fixing, making a fiction of the so-called open-market concept—is but half the picture of current private capitalism. The nation has become a war state with its best technology, its best resources, its best ingenuity and human resources geared to death and destruction. The extent of the "military-industrial complex"—which we were warned against by the late President Eisenhower in his farewell address on January 17, 1961—is pointedly covered by citing several paragraphs of a speech of Senator Stephen Young of Ohio on the Senate floor on March 24, 1969. He had this to say:

Mr. President, the United States today is the world's largest military-industrial complex. Our Armed Forces total more than 3,606,000 men. We have more than 6,000 military bases within our borders. More than 1,531,000 American servicemen are stationed in more than 350 additional installations in Western Europe, Asia, Africa and throughout the entire world.

Ten percent of the American labor is involved in either military or related employment. Approximately 22,000 of our largest manufacturing corporations are prime military contractors, while more than 100,000 firms contribute some type of output to defense production.

The United States is the world's largest exporter of munitions. Our annual expenditures for defense purposes, so-called, far exceed the total amount spent for welfare, education and poverty programs.

Still, the pressures of the military-industrial complex for costlier, more intricate defense systems go on—the most recent examples being the proposed ABM system, which will cost anywhere from $6 billion to more than $100 billion and be obsolete before completion, as were all missile systems already constructed at a cost of more than $19 billion.

Meanwhile, most of our cities, where approximately 70 percent of our population live, are suffering and in deep trouble. Some of the largest have been termed dying cities. Crime, congestion, squalor, misery and pollution of the air our people breathe are prevalent in nearly every American city. There are shameful slum areas which should no longer be tolerated. At the same time, the military-industrial establishment is given a virtual blank check for more guns and more armaments with hardly a serious thought given as to whether these are actually needed for our defense.

A few pages couldn't commence to give an adequate picture of the all-encompassing Moloch of Carnage that the nation has become. Books, congressional investigation and independent research abound covering the criminal waste—both in material and human life—since World War II. During that time **1.4 trillion taxpayers dollars** have been spent on "defense" and currently the colossal waste continues with an expenditure of $80 billion is annually. Of that annual amount $44 billion is spent of defense procurement, equivalent to about 25 percent of the Federal budget, which is divided up amongst the nation's largest corporation.

Today the Department of Defense controls 45,000 squares miles of land in this country, exceeding the land area of the State of Pennsylvania, and has land holdings exceeding $200 billion. And in addition to the 3,600,000 in military uniform, the Department of Defense and the military uniform, the Department of Defense and the military have employed nearly 1,000,000 civilian employees.

It is this huge war establishment coupled with the 100 top industrial firms and their subsidiaries—which received $26.2 billion in prime contracts in 1968, 67 percent of the total—that in the main make up the military-industrial complex.

As this is being written a Report entitled "The Economics of Military Procurement" has been publicly released by the Subcommittee on Economy in Government, of the Joint Economic Committee of the Congress, dated May, 1969. A few excerpts are indicated because they highlight the privilege enjoyed by the large corporations in all war contracts.

Under the sub-title "Economic Inefficiency and Waste" the following few lines show the inherent waste in the whole defense boondoggle:

The extensive and pervasive economic inefficiency and waste that occurs in the military procurement program has been well documented by the investigation of this subcommittee ... literally billions of dollars have been wasted on weapons systems that have had to be canceled because they did not work . . . For example, one study referred to in the hearings shows that of a sample of 13 major Air Force and Navy aircraft and missile programs initiated since 1955 at a total cost of $40 billion, less than 40 percent produced systems with acceptable electronic performance. Two of the programs were canceled after total program costs of $2 billion were paid. Two programs costing $10 billion were phased out after 3 years for low reliability. Five programs costing $13 billion give poor performance; that is, their electronic reliability is less than 75 percent of initial specifications.

Under the sub-title "Low competition and high concentration" we note the following:

Defense buying practices are reducing competition for Government contracts and increasing economic concentration within the defense industry. Formally advertised competitive military contract dollar awards dropped from 13.4 percent in fiscal year 1967 to 11.5 percent in fiscal year 1968. Single source procurement increased to 57.9 percent . . .

Department of Defense procurement is highly concentrated. A relatively small number of contractors receive most of the dollar value of defense awards. In fiscal year 1968, the 100 largest defense contractors were awarded 67.4 percent of total defense contracts, the highest percentage since 1965.

Under the sub-title "Government-owned property" is revealed the fact that the taxpayers are underwriting billions of dollars in free equipment:

In addition to the lack of competition for defense contracts, the Defense Department's policy of providing Government-owned property and working capital to defense contractors constitutes a Government subsidy and contributes to concentration within this industry. The cost of Government-owned equipment supplied to contractors sometimes exceeds the value of property owned by the company. While the total value of Government-owned property in the hands of contractors declined from $14.6 billion in fiscal year 1967 to $13.3 billion in fiscal year 1968, reflecting primarily a drop in the amount of materials, in the important category of industrial plant equipment costing over $1,000 there was an increase from $2.6 billion to $2.7 billion. A disproportionate amount of this equipment was held by the large contractors.

However, it is not just material and equipment that is furnished free as a special privilege to the large corporations. Under the sub-title "Progress payments" is revealed the fact that they enjoy interest-free capital working capital:

The Pentagon makes so-called progress payments to reimburse contractors for up to 90 percent of incurred costs, on a pay-as-you-go basis . . . . It is possible, for example, for a contractor to incur costs equal to 75 percent of the original contract price while completing only 50 percent, or less, of the job . . . The important point is that the payments are made interest-free, prior to completion or delivery of the end-product. The contractor could operate largely without his own working capital, on capital supplied by the Federal Government, particularly in expensive, long leadtime procurement . . . Contractors so favored have a sizeable competitive advantage over others in the defense and civilian industries, and are actually highly subsidized . . . Money advanced to contractors in the form of progress payments are really no-interest Government loans which inflate contractor's profits. Armed with free working capital a contractor may be able to bid low for more Government work, "finance" commercial work, or otherwise compete unfairly in the commercial market.

Finally, we should extract from the Report the advantages enjoyed by the large corporations in obtaining exclusive patent rights:

The Government's patent policy similarly tends to reduce competition and increase the concentration and increase the concentration of economic power. Briefly, the Government permits contractors to obtain exclusive patent rights, free of charge, on inventions produced in the performance of Government contracts . . . The contractor, in other words, obtains a monopoly which he can exploit for his own private gain in the commercial market for inventions paid for by public moneys. This "fringe benefit" of doing business under Government contracts does not get reported as part of the contractor's profits. In effect, the public pays twice. Once through the Government contract; again in the marketing of the private monopoly.

In should be noted that the contractor's own patent policy differs from that of the Department of Defense. When contractors award contracts to independent research institutes, the contractors, not the research institutes, retain the patent rights. Further, the employees of contractors generally must agree that the contractor gets the patent rights to any inventions developed during their employment.

. . . one half of the patents acquired by contractors as a result of Government-financed research and development work are owned by 20 large corporations . . . the very same companies that receive the lion's share of contracts.

The foregoing excerpts from the Report by the Subcommittee on Economy in Government, headed Senator William Proximire, reveal the special privilege enjoyed by the giant corporations in a war economy. Add these privileges to the conventional advantages enjoyed by the monopolies in the whole spectrum of price-fixing and one can better understand how a continuous "hot" and "cold" war environment has explosively concentrated the assets of the nation and accentuated the "disastrous rise of misplaced power" warned against by President Eisenhower some eight years ago.

Military-industrial-financial-political Complex

However, this war-oriented entity of a military-industrial complex is not some isolated entity either in drive or makeup. Part and parcel, interwoven and interrelated with it are the nation's private political institutions and the nation's private banking institutions. Structurally, it is more accurate to state that a "military-industrial-financial-political" complex has risen in our midst.

During the entire history of this nation, particularly during the larger part of the current century, concerned people have recognized that private capitalism by its very nature gave rise to the exercise of abnormal power. However, not having documented evidence at hand as to who wielded the real power in the nation, even the reasonably enlightened were all too often forced to refer to the "rich" or the "ruling class" or the "invisible government" in identifying despotic and monopolistic control in the society. No longer is it necessary to use such vague terms. Documentary evidence now exists to surfeit in identifying the oligarchic forces, and their executive personnel, that really control the nation.

When we speak of "the system" we are speaking of the whole structured military-industrial-financial-political complex which creates the environment in which the total people live and endeavor to work out their well-being. When we speak of the dominating institutions within that system, we can identify them as follows:

1. Military—The Department of Defense with $200 billion in property holdings, its over 4,500,000 military and civilian employees, and its annual budget of $80 billion.

2. Industrial (and services)—the largest industrial plants, 50 largest retailers, 50 largest utilities, 50 largest insurance companies, and 50 largest transportation companies.

3. Financial—the 100 largest commercial banks and the Federal Reserve System which the private banks own and control

4. Political—the two major political parties and the Congress.

It is the foregoing interlocking and interrelated complex of artificial entities that own, dominate, direct and determine the economic, political and social life of the nation's 200,000,000 citizens. It is this complex that has brought about a circumstance where crime is increasing faster than the increase in population. It is this complex that has brought about a circumstance where indebtedness is increasing faster than the increase in productivity.

It is this complex that controls directly or indirectly the nation's communication media—radio, television and newspapers—and prevents the people from knowing the underlying causes of the nation's plight. It is this complex that controls directly or indirectly the nation's educational institutions which shape the minds of the young to accept the status quo of the society. It is this complex that controls directly or indirectly the makeup of the nation's halls of state and thereby are the real arbiters both of making the nation's laws and of the executing of those laws.

Yes, it is the influences and dictates of the power structures—military, production, money and politics—that have led to a circumstance where millions of our children suffer from malnutrition, millions break mentally from the pressures of the society, millions are doomed to a life of illiteracy and millions die needlessly from lack of medical care. Most seriously, it is the influences and dictates of these power structures that have created and perpetual circumstance where the nation's best manhood are needlessly sacrificed in wars.

The American people are compelled to make the horrifying conclusion that to such an extent is the whole economy dependent on war production for employment, and to such an extent is the war production a lucrative venture for the giant corporations, and to such an extent is the war production a political patronage bonanza that actual peace is unwanted, at least unwittingly, by those who are the beneficiaries of the spoils of war. How much longer can this nation be witness to the finest in the land being brought home in coffins that the coffers of the callous and the greedy might be heavily laden?

How much longer can a military-industrial-financial-political complex be tolerated which has stockpiled a poison-gas and nuclear arsenal that if deliberately or accidentally fused would destroy all mankind and make the planet uninhabitable?

Belatedly, it must be recognized that the strides the nation made technologically were made in spite of the system of private capitalism. As we have tried to portray throughout this book, the economic history of this nation has been the systematic process of fewer and fewer artificial entities being able to siphon off more and more of the real wealth of the nation to the final stultifying of the whole economic system. It has been the law of the jungle in the nation's economy. It has been the constant triumph of profits, property, power and privilege over the vast majority of toiling, striving, struggling and aspiring human beings.

Only those who do not want to face reality are unable to see that the inevitable result of accelerated trends is an economy monopolized by the few and for the few which will drive out of existence any place for the majority of workers and the small operators. What chance have the millions of workers when they can be replaced by machines? What chance has the small farmer or the small manufacturer to compete with in corporate entities employing the most modern technology and enjoying privileged legislation? What chance has the small retailer endeavoring to compete with giant corporate supermarkets?

The tens of millions of workers, consumers and taxpayers in the nation have become the robot slaves of an economic and social system that has thrived on disadvantaging the people. It is a system of creating the vacuums into which bureaucracy, welfarism, indebtedness, war and finally the police state move to make up for the system's gross inefficiencies.

It is a system of Twentieth Century feudalism more reprehensible than medieval feudalism, for the serfs of that distant day knew they were slaves, and today the people are unaware of the cause of their economic slavery.

It is a system of dual slavery—both economic and political.

Chapter 17

POLITICAL PARTIES VS THE SOVEREIGN PEOPLE

ERRONEOUSLY, MANY AMERICANS believe that political parties were provided for in the Constitution. There is no such provision. In fact, the first political convention was not held until 1831. Secondly, few are the people who recognize that there is nothing sacrosanct about the "two-party" system, that this political concept has been deliberately promoted by the power blocs in our society who by financing and controlling both major parties can preclude all threats to their ill-gotten gains and usurped power.

In short, the formula for taking over any people is first to get control of a nation's issuance of money, then corral all of its industrial assets, and finally through these monopolies underwrite all major political candidates who will be beholden to act at the monopolist's dictation.

Over-simplified, this is the pattern of political slavery. Unfortunately, it is the fate that has befallen America.

By and large, with few exceptions, the men and women who hold political office, on every level of government, are those who have been carefully screened by the economic and financial "establishments" that wield absolute power on every stratum of our society. The people have had no meaningful role in their selection. It should not be difficult to realize that such selected political officeholders are not only the lackeys of those who made their election possible but at the same time have become entrapped themselves in defending economic injustice that their own political opportunism might be insured. In many cases, such politicians are more to be pitied than condemned.

The strength, organizational potential and domination of the two political parties are derived by massive underwriting from those who **already** have economic advantage. Secondly, by the instrument of **patronage** there exists both economic and political pay-offs to insure the existence and longevity of both parties, and the status quo of the socio economic system.

Deception of Two-Party System

First, let us consider this holier-than-holy concept of the so-called "two-party" system. To hear the proponents and apologists defend such system one would think that the whole idea had been delivered on tablets of gold by angelic messenger. In fact, anyone brash enough to question its divine quality is quickly charged with blasphemy and promoting anarchy. It is all a ruse to protect the usurpers of authority.

Of course, the defender of the two major political parties will offer plausible reasons for their existence. He will tell you that they make possible divergent points of view and thus the electorate has a choice in voting for candidates. Theoretically, this seems convincing. In practice, it is quite different. Such theory is but a smokescreen blinding the people to the irrefutable fact that **both** candidates are selected by multi-million dollar machines that are but fronts for the other power structures in our society. Even on the local level, the local "establishment" exercises the prevailing voice.

More serious, of course, is the circumstance that the elected candidate has assumed no obligation to speak for the people but is beholden to those who nominated him and underwrote his campaign. Political parties, as they function in this nation, are interlocking monopolies with the commands of the top sifting down to the lowliest precinct.

The whole promotion of the two-party system concept is to trick the people into believing they have a choice in political leadership when in reality such acceptance is sheer deception.

To those possessing economic power, it is absolute insurance in protecting their pilfered wealth and in perpetuating the economic-financial system that is responsible for their economic domination.

National Conventions

To the enlightened there is no more sickening demonstration in the sacred name of a "free society" than national political conventions. From the first sound of the gavel to the final swish of the janitor's broom, such conventions are an insult to any rational person. In sheer hypocrisy and sham, they have no equal. What is disturbing, of course, is the fact that they represent the political mechanics by which are chosen the men to hold the two highest offices in our government.

Political conventions! Let's recognize them for the subterfuge they are. They are the Twentieth Century's replica of the Roman Circus. Behind all the trappings, the hoopla and discordant sounds, the histrionics of arm-waving and patriotic vaporings, the confusion and the milling of delegates, behind all these is the feeding of the America electorate to the lions of political intrigue and of political double-cross.

Payola of Patronage

The glue that holds the whole conglomerate of political usurpation together is patronage. This has been the spoils that has bought and sold votes throughout the political history of this nation. It has been the political pay-offs to those who worked for and took orders from the party machines. From the operating of the local license bureau by the County Chairman (as in some States) to the appointing of postmasters, to the recommending of judgeships, to the awarding of hundreds of billions of tax-dollars in public project and war contracts, all major political parties have employed and do employ patronage to perpetuate their existence through enforced political allegiance.

The result is that elected candidates are in the business of making political pay-offs, particularly in kowtowing to the dictates of the billion-dollar lobbyists, and are not in the business of reflecting the rights and interests of the people. When such political pay-offs lessen the well-being of the whole citizenry—not only in the blocking of social change needed for economic justice within our own borders, but in the sending of America's best manhood to die in foreign wars in the defense of the political and economic interests of the propertied blocs— then the whole political arrangement is not only intolerable but criminal.

The following excerpts from a speech by Senator Russell Long on April 4, 1967 when he was Majority Whip unabashedly reveals that Members of Congress move at the behest of the corporate interests who are the chief contributors to their political campaigns:

> Because of the high cost of campaigning and the inability of most candidates to pay the cost themselves, every corporation, every vested interest, every monopoly, every businessman in America, particularly the large and wealthy ones, have a virtual standing invitation to contribute large sums of money and in return to receive assurances of one sort or another that they will receive a sympathetic ear.
>
> Here is where the big corporations, acting through their executives, have the opportunity to gain assurance that monopolies will not be upset radically, that appointees to regulatory agencies will be acceptable to those whom they are supposed to regulate, that the wealthy will continue to enjoy tax loopholes.

Conflict of Interests

No greater insight into the operation of the Congress of the United States is obtained than to have knowledge of the stockholdings, assets and interests which each member possesses. It should be obvious that to the degree any member has a financial interest in any corporation, to that same degree he will be disposed to vote in his own self-interest. Not only is he disposed to fatten his own holdings, but in too many cases he is obligated to the monopolists in finance and industry who directly or indirectly made his election possible. Billion-dollar lobbyists have little trouble dictating legislation if their own stockholders introduce and enact the laws.

All attempts to pass a "disclosure of holdings law have been thwarted by the overriding majority of Congressmen who want no disclosure of their tie-ins with the monopolies of finance and industry. Of course, a number of conscientious members of both Houses have disclosed their assets and holdings. What is revealing is that the few who have submitted certified statements, such as Senator Young of Ohio and Senator Proxmire of Wisconsin, have each occupied columns of the **Congressional Record** in order to list their numerous holdings in major corporations, in real estate, in stocks and in bonds. One can only speculate as to the undoubtedly much, much larger holdings of other members of Congress who refuse to make such a financial statement.

The publicized fact that the Senate alone contains upwards of 30 millionaires in its ranks should leave little doubt as to the conflicts of interests that exist. This fact alone should erase any contention that the ordinary citizens, especially the 52% of the entire population who as individual households own total assets of only $1800 each, have any meaningful representation in Washington.

Seniority and Senility

Nothing is more puerile than for those seeking social justice to believe that Congress, on its own initiative, will make major renovations toward unleashing the nation's productive potential and in creating a good life for all citizens. The reason for the indisposition to consider changes in society can be found beyond the political screening by the propertied entities who direct the political parties. It goes beyond the circumstance that the majority of the members of Congress are economically tied into the monopolistic makeup of the economy, either as stockholders or recipients of government contracts.

The inability to get major social change commensurate with the nation's capability in this new technological age, and the inability to achieve peace, is due to the crystallized structure of the Congress itself. Over many decades the Congress has developed political hierarchies within its own framework that perpetuate a constant defense of the entire military-industrial-financial complex.

The key to this gradient hierarchy is the **seniority system**. The heart of this system is the chairmanships. In the House of Representatives there are 20 chairmen and in the Senate there are 16 chairmen. These **36** chairmen rule with the power of little despots. They have the arbitrary power of little despots. They have the arbitrary power to determine what legislation will come out of committees and what legislation will be indefinitely stalled. In their hands exists a dictatorial power that makes a farce of the democratic process.

The minimum qualification is that they have fed at the public trough the longest. Seniority in itself testifies to the fact that the power structures have displayed a consistent willingness to promote the re-election of the "tried and seasoned" chairmen. However, the chairmen have played no small role in promoting their own re-election. Their propensity for steering the larger war contracts and government appropriations to their own areas has assured their perpetuity in office.

This is not to say, particularly in cases like Senator Hart, Proxmire and Fulbright, and Representative Wright Patman, that some chairman have not risen above the demands of the privileged and responsibly discharged their office. But these men are the exceptions to the rule, and even they give little indication that they are disposed to promote any major restructuring of the society.

As to a newly elected member of Congress, however eager and desirous of performing constructively, he finds he must compromise lest he forgo all chance of getting re-elected. Even constituents won't send back members who somehow are unable to get their share of Federal tax-dollars. Anyway, for the first full year, every new Congressman usually abides by the unwritten law that he be inactive until he is oriented to the political hierarchies that dominate the Congress.

No one wishes to criticize old age. But when advancing years measure the length of time men have either passively or aggressively compromised their people and their nation, it is something else. What then of the fact that in 1968 of the 36 chairmen of both the House and Senate, the average age was 67 years old, and 13 chairmanships were occupied by men over 70? How is it possible to speak of representative government, with over half of the population under 25 years old, when all the important positions of Congress are filled by men of a fading generation?

At a time when new ideas and new concepts are needed to solve our problems, senility has been placed on the political pedestal as the chief qualification for leadership. No wonder the young, making up the majority of the population, have no political communication with those who purport to represent them. Conversely, is it any wonder that the politician of a bygone era can't "dig" the young and the new approaches needed in a technological age?

The Pentagon

The Pentagon, constructed in the early 1940's, at a cost of $50 million for the building alone, is the so-called "nerve center" for the mightiest military machine in the world. It is in this fort-like structure that the Secretary of Defense, the members of the Joint Chiefs of Staff, and more than 26,000 employees (civilian and military), carry out the military involvements and the military spending of the nation. It is this centralized military establishment that has spent the sum of $1.4 trillion since World War II and has given identity to the "military-industrial complex" covered in the preceding chapter.

What concerns us is that during the span of some 25 years the military, the nation's largest industries and the Congress have become so interdependent on each other that the people's representatives have become but a tool of big business and the military. Thus, not only are the most serious social problems neglected but we are witness to prolonged war, with all the exacting and tragic costs in blood and materiel, in order that the self-interest of the military establishment and the giant corporations might be served.

It is only when we grasp the overriding circumstance that the whole war-orientation of society is the final gasp of private capitalism to survive that we can understand how our political institution have become the captive agents of the military-industrial complex whose existence is dependent on perpetuation of a stained-in-blood war economy. Perhaps the simple fact that in 1968 the average American was taxed $402.08 for arms, while that same American was taxed only $2.52 to provide food and care for his fellow citizens, markedly attests to the fact that we are not a welfare state but a warfare state.

There is no problem in showing the military influence as to personnel in both industry and the Congress. Of recent time much publicity has been to the fact that as of February, 1969 some 2,072 retired military officers of the rank of colonel or Navy captain and above were employed by the 100 largest military contractors. It should be readily apparent that these military officers, now in the pay of industry, have special entrée to the Pentagon and are instrumental in getting the largest industries the largest volume of prime military contracts. The evidence speaks for itself. In the fiscal year 1968, the 100 largest companies got $26.2 billion or 67.4 percent.

In considering the makeup of Congress itself, it is pertinent to note that Congress had 32 senators and 107 representatives, or one member of Congress out of every four, who were commissioned officers either in the standby or retired categories. Many of these military men such as Democrat Senator Howard Cannon and Republican Senator Strom Thurmond, major generals in the Air Force and Army Reserve, are members of the most important military committees.

However, it is not only that Congress itself contains so many members that have military backgrounds, many of these seated on committees dealing with the Pentagon, but seniority has placed at the head of both the Senate and House Committees of Armed Services and on Appropriations men, all southerners, who have shown a supine disposition to acquiesce to the demands of the military establishment. These four committee chairmen, each with over 20 years in the Congress, are part of the southern hierarchy. They are as follows:

Mendel Rivers of South Carolina, 63, a congressman for 28 years, chairman of the House Armed Services Committee. George Mahon of Texas, 68, a congressman for 38 years, chairman of the House Appropriations Committee. John Stennis of Mississippi, 67, a senator for 21 years, chairman of the Senate Armed Forces Committee. Richard Russell of Georgia, 71, the senior member of the Senate with 36 years of service, and chairman of the Senate Appropriations Committee.

It is these four chairmen who rule with an iron hand, whose key meetings are held behind locked doors, and who head the committees that approve the proposals of the military and in turn approve the billions in appropriations to be dished out by the Pentagon. It is pertinent to note that during the 14-year period between 1951 and 1965 these committees made available more than $357 billion in appropriations for war contracts and that of that amount 86.3 percent, or $307 billion, was not put out on bids but was handled through negotiated procurement. It is no surprise to observe that senators and congressmen heading important committees such as the Armed Services and Appropriations are from states which receive the largest amounts.

The perspective that must be gained is that the whole nation has become so war-oriented, with one out of every ten Americans working for a living in some aspect of the nation's defense establishment, some 22,000 major defense contractors, with 15 of the top 38 of these from 1961 to 1967 getting more than half their business from military contracts, that Congress has become vulnerable to the threats of serious economic breakdown if it refuses to vote billions upon billions of taxpayers' dollars to keep the largest defense plants operating. According to the 1968 **Congressional Quarterly**, which listed the 991 largest privately owned defense plants and government-owned installations, each state had at least one such large plant or installation and so did 363 of the 435 congressional districts.

Congress Is Captive Agent

The Congress of the United States has become a captive agent of the military-industrial-financial power structures in the society. No longer does it as a body reflect the needs or wishes of the electorate. In perpetuating a war economy, the Congress has placed its offices and the taxpayers' hard work on the side of the directors and profiteers of private capitalism. In such role, even those members who see the wrongness of our involvement in the Vietnam War, feel compelled to vote for appropriations that in turn prolong our brutal and illegal participation in that tragic war.

The American people, in the Vietnam War alone, have seen 35,000 of their finest boys slaughtered on the battlefield with another 200,000 wounded, many without legs or hands or eyes for the rest of their lives. On May 14, 1966, General David M. Shoup, Commander of all U. S. Marine forces in Vietnam from 1960 to 1963, had this to say to students at Pierce College, Los Angeles:

> I want to tell you, I don't think the whole of Southeast Asia, as related to the present and future safety and freedom of the people of this country, is worth the life or limb of a single American. I believe that if we had and would keep our dirty, dollar-crooked fingers out of the business of these nations so full of depressed, exploited people, they will arrive at a solution of their own. That they will sign and want. That they fight and work for. If unfortunately their revolution must be of the violent type because the "haves" refuse to share with the "have-nots" by any peaceful method, at least what they will get will be their own, and not American style, which they don't want and above all don't want crammed down their throats by Americans.

The same yardstick should be applied to private capitalism. To paraphrase General Shoup, the whole of private capitalism, as related to the present and future safety and freedom of the people of this country, is not worth the life or limb of one American, and if the power structures would keep their dirty, dollar-crooked fingers out of the business of the people, the people would arrive at a solution of their own. One which they design and want. And if unfortunately the people's revolution must be of the violent type because the "haves" refuse to share with the "have-nots" by any peaceful method, at least what they get will be their own, and not the private-capitalist style, which they do not want and above all, don't want crammed down their throats by conscienceless profiteers.

The nation's politicians should give heed to General Shoup's assessment both as it applies to Vietnam and as it can be applied to the oppressed and exploited of our own nation—and all nations for that matter.

Chapter 18

"ABSOLUTE POWER CORRUPTS ABSOLUTELY!"

A CONSIDERABLE number of pages have been devoted to portraying the inherent flaws of private capitalism and the compounding of those flaws, resulting in the current dilemma of the nation. If we have presented clearly what has happened to this nation, three obvious circumstances should stand out:

1. The well-being, the security and the self-reliance of human beings have not been in direct ratio to the nation's progressive advancements in tools, in technology and in scientific knowledge.

2. The main thrust of the whole socio-economic-financial-political system has been the expanding profits, growth and power of artificial entities at the expense of the inherent rights and betterment of human beings.

3. Indebtedness, bureaucracy, militarism and violence are the inescapable denouements of a "system" geared to the exploitation and control of a nation's assets and its citizens.

However, a fourth circumstance needs to be emphasized. Interwoven throughout, and part of, all the foregoing circumstances has been the **corrupting influence of power.** What must be recognized is that private capitalism from the beginning has been a contest for unlimited assets and unlimited control of human beings. With no holds barred, each person went out into the national arena to fend for himself, the stronger and more cunning strangling and incapacitating the weaker.

Viewed in retrospect, what blindness for a people to have tolerated an economic and political environment within which control, compounding control, underlay all human relationships!

What sheer madness to have set up offices throughout every aspect of society that appealed to man's possessive drives instead of his inner potential for creative work and a natural capacity to be of service to others!

In 1959 a book was published entitled "Power and Morality." Its authors were the late Pitirim Sorokin, Professor at Harvard and Walter A. Lunden, Professor of Sociology at Iowa State University. The research for the book was supported by Mr. Eli Lilly and the Lilly Endowment, a previous bequest from whom had led to the establishment of the Harvard Research Center in Creative Altruism in 1949, which Professor Sorokin directed.

The important contribution that these distinguished professors have made, and it should be noted that both are learned men with many years of research and writing in the fields of sociology and criminality, is to historically substantiate Lord Acton's classic statement, "Power corrupts, and absolute power corrupts absolutely." Covering the past twenty-five centuries of Greco-Roman and Western civilization, they show that to the exact degree that power is exercised, to that same degree criminal behavior is present. The whole spectrum of crime, from bribery and fraud to killing and mass murder, is covered. No aspect, or level, of society is untainted by the corrupting influence of power.

Out of the whole research, which cites not only statistics of crime but relates them directly to persons and offices, emerges the irrefutable picture that the tendency toward, and the guilt of, crime are overwhelmingly more prevalent in those who **rule** than in the **ruled**.

Although increased power corrupts men, whether in industry, finance, or even in institutionalized religions the most naked and irresponsible display of power is in governments themselves. Here we find that criminality has always exceeded that of the rank and file who have made up the citizenry. Every level of government is affected.

Whereas we readily associate brutality, chicanery and murder with pre-Western despotic rulers, most people are blind to the fact that outside of the larger part of the Nineteenth Century, when a reasonable degree of democratic participation existed both economically and politically, the nations of the world have reverted back to a condition of immorality and violence making the bestiality of the past insignificant by comparison.

In their introduction to "Power and Morality," the authors state:

> Never before in history has the life or death of so many depended upon so very few! The greatest autocrats of the past had but a fraction of the tremendous power held now by a few members of the Politburo or the top leaders of the United States ruling elite. This dangerous situation naturally raises the momentous questions of our time: Can we entrust the fateful decision of war or peace—and through that the "life, liberty and pursuit happiness" of hundreds of millions of human beings—to the few magnates of this power? Do they have the wisdom of the serpent and the innocence of the dove necessary to lead us to a lasting peace and a magnificent future?

Authors Sorokin and Lunden answer their own questions with these succinct conclusions:

> Still mainly tribal governments of politicians, by politicians, and for politicians, today's ruling groups do not display the minimum of intellectual, moral and social qualifications necessary for a successful solution of these tremendous tasks . . . Throughout history the moral integrity of powerful governments has been— and still is—too low and their criminality too great to entrust to them the life and well-being of mankind.

The authors have presented a historically supported thesis that "power corrupts, and absolute power corrupts absolutely."

190

They also urgently plead for complete disarmament, fully recognizing the suicidal threat of a thermo-nuclear holocaust, and logically urge the adoption of an "Integral" order amongst mankind, premised on love instead of hate.

"Systems" that must be indicted

Those who have read carefully what we have offered to this point are aware that our chief emphasis has been on indicting systems as systems. We have stressed unequivocally that it is the very nature of Capitalism to concentrate power in fewer and fewer hands with larger and larger segments of the population denied both equity in and enjoyment of the nation's increased ability to produce all goods and services to abundance.

We have not minced words in labeling such a society a slave society, with the spoils going to those who wield abnormal and abusive power.

Although it is specific individuals who exercise corrupt and criminal power, the basic wrong lies with the system which permits and encourages the exercise of corruption and exploitation. Ultimately the whole society degenerates into an unstable condition with complete breakdown in the offing.

All levels of society have become victims. All are losers. The few have been corrupted by **over-participation.** The majority are increasingly driven to crime and anti-social conduct because of **under-participation**.

We have made a specific point of not over-concerning ourselves with indicting personalities. We see the folly and futility of concentrating on individuals or groups, however criminal their actions. They appear and disappear with the passing of time but the faulty system persists through each succeeding generation. Our indictment must single out the social, economic and political arrangement itself which methodically and diabolically does its best to make criminals of all within its jurisdiction.

An analogy would be a car with faulty steering mechanism. It should be apparent that whatever the skill of the driver, or his innate virtues, he will careen down the highway, endangering or taking the lives of innocent bystanders and inevitably end up in collision. Increase the horsepower of the engine and you simply compound the potential for irresponsibility and criminal behavior on the part of the driver.

So it has been with the nation. Capitalism, camouflaged by such terms as "free enterprise" and "equal opportunity" has been a national vehicle without a constructively engineered steering mechanism. It has been a system which gives privileged drivers the right to ride roughshod over anybody and everybody who questions or opposes oligarchic domination. It has been a system which postulates that the ability to take advantage of people, to extort unearned tributes, and to perpetuate war economies together with unlimited sacrifice of American lives, carries with it the moral justification of all such dastardly acts.

Capitalism, like Communism, is a power-structure system and is unworkable. Neither system respects the dignity of the individual and his inherent right to be a sovereign participant in working out his own well-being. In both systems, power begets power and with it progressive corruption. The only differentiation is that under Communism the political oligarchy runs the nation economically while under Capitalism the industrial-military-financial oligarchy runs the nation politically.

Both systems have double standards of morality in the administration of justice.

Double Standards of Law and Morality

Any person who makes a serious business of analyzing existing conditions in the nation is quick to discover a circumstance that permeates all levels of society. This circumstance is apparent irrespective of which facet of human relationships is considered. It is simply this: **There is one set of laws or code for moral behavior for those who possess power and there is another set and code for the majority who must move at the behest of those who administer that power.**

This double standard of both law and morality presents challenges that cannot be ignored by those who seek equity in all social structures.

Only the extremely naive and gullible don't recognize the foregoing circumstance. Yet, such observation by the majority only encompasses a surface recognition. The average citizen is only aware that if one has money, plenty of that green stuff, or if one occupies high position in any power structure, or if one knows the right people, one can commit "murder" and get away with it.

On the other hand, if one is just an ordinary, struggling, tax-paying citizen, he can be sent to prison for merely stealing a five-gallon can of gasoline or failing to pay confiscatory taxes. However, the magnitude of the injustices and dangers inherent in all areas of concentrated power is beyond his knowledge.

In our own nation nothing sickens the heart so much as to see the double standards of justice that maintain between those who wield power and the ordinary citizens.

No sane person can condone stealing or bodily injury by anyone, even though in the case of a father we can understand his desperation and uncontrollable urge to steal from the abundance denied him that he might provide necessities for his family. Yet, what then of an economic order that has its underlying premise the right of those forces dominating the economy to chisel or "steal" from the majority to the extent that a whole nation has become hopelessly indebted and forty millions of its citizens pauperized? Is there any real significance whether the weapon is called a gun or whether the weapons are **exorbitant profits** and **fictitious credit** wielded by giant monopolies and the privately owned banking system?

In the first instance we have laws that make robbery a crime while in the second instance we have accepted economic theory or passed laws that legalized the sacking of an entire nation. Certainly the lesser of the two crimes is that of the unemployed father who even at gunpoint demands the bank's cash that he might feed his hungry kids.

Frankly, we see no difference in the solitary thug's waylaying a law-abiding citizen and dealing him a fatal blow that his wallet might be taken, and a society's denying its citizens the necessary food to sustain life, that the greed of monopolists might be satisfied.

We have a become a nation which has one set of rules governing the conduct of the ordinary citizen and another set of rules governing the exploiters or most powerful forces in society. There is one set of laws for the little fellow. There is another set of laws for the big fellow. The citizen who robs the local filling station gets fifteen years in prison while the private banking system and corporate cartels rob millions of people of hundreds of billions of dollars through usury, fictitious credit, and price-fixing and they are sanctified as being in harmony with our "free enterprise" system. The small wage earner hands over a third of his earnings to the tax collector while the millionaire too often doesn't pay a dime because he can always find a loophole or pass the tax down to those below him.

Certainly no one condones the taking of another person's life. But, we ask, what logic or code of morality upholds the sending of one individual to prison for life because he commits murder and at the same time does not condemn and punish economic and political power blocs who murder through promoted wars? Is murder less murder because it is done in uniform or those slaughtered are of a different skin color?

Does the magnitude of criminal violence lessen the guilt of the perpetrator? Or the fact that the triggering is done by government oligarchies instead of individuals?

Complete Dispersal of Power

There can be only one code of morality and one standard of justice for all people. This can only be achieved by making those who now wield abusive and criminal power to disgorge such immoral power. Recognizing that power corrupts the few at the top who then proceed to disadvantage the majority at the bottom, the only hope for humanity lies in dispersing power back into the hands of all the people where it inherently belongs.

The key to a just and safe society is the complete dispersal of power throughout all society. Such dispersal would not only eliminate the corrupting influence of power but more importantly it would restore to each individual his inherent right to be decision-making participant in shaping his life and his future.

Let us in the in the next chapter consider the fundamental makeup of social contracts and constitutions so that we can understand the basic premises upon which all social reform—both political and economic—must be based in arriving at solutions.

In the follow-up chapters we will deal specifically with the major social reform that must come to pass if the nation is to survive and the people are to derive meaningful purpose from their lives.

Chapter 19

SOCIAL CONTRACTS

NINE-TENTHS of the difficulty in getting people to understand the problems of the nation and the solutions that could be adopted is that they don't have a fundamental grasp of the basic ingredients that should make up organized society. Only the rare person keeps in the forefront of his thinking that there is no such thing as a government of and by itself. He grasps that constitutions, which provide for the setting up of governments, are always **agreements among people and none other.**

The informed person on governments is therefore astounded and perplexed by the conservatives who see "red"—fiery red—when it is emphasized that the full and absolute decision-making power is vested, and can only be vested, in the hands of all the people. The minute that one is brash enough to suggest that the corrupting influence of power can only be eliminated by restoring the full power to the people; one is confronted with such retorts as "mobocracy" and "mediocrity." Or there is much said about this nation's being set up as a republic" and not a "democracy."

This whole subject of power, decision-making power, and who should exercise it, deserves much analysis because it lies at the heart of all the major problems of organized society. We cannot deal adequately with the subject here but some basic thinking can be presented for consideration.

Let us commence by setting up the simplest society. Suppose that a shipload of 100 passengers becomes marooned on an isolated island and by sheer circumstance must work out all their economic, social and political relationships. The obvious thing happens. They gather in council and hold a town meeting.

Before opening the meeting even for discussion, a cardinal point should be recognized: **The desire and will to arrive at agreements rests solely with the people themselves.**

The reason this point is so important is that after rules and agreements have been reached, whether they are called contracts or constitutions, a tendency arises to subordinate the people to the agreement without recognizing that only as the agreement expresses the will of the people is it valid and commands obedience. Social contracts, in terms of 100 islanders or a nation such as the United States, are agreements among people and none other.

Both the inviolate power to bring them into being and the power to change them rests with the people.

It is inconceivable that any rational individual, unless coerced, would join in an agreement that would disservice him or disadvantage him. Nor would any rational individual join in an agreement that didn't allow him full opportunity to have equal voice in persuading others in modification of the agreement. This brings us to a second cardinal point: **Social contracts and constitutions are agreed to by their participants solely because they protect equally the self-interest of every individual.**

In considering the circumstance of our marooned 100 islanders, it should be immediately apparent that the self-interest of every person would involve two specific areas. It would involve the individual's right to equal access to the raw stock of nature, and it would involve every individual's right to expend unlimited effort toward the building of that person's desired standard of living. Let us consider them separately.

A hundred people finding themselves on an isolated island would get the full impact of the fact that the trees, the soil, the minerals and rocks, the water—all that which nature has provided—belonged to all equally. There would be immediate agreement that every islander should have equal access to the trees to build his house and warm it, to the beasts and the fowl and the soil to provide for both his food and clothing, and to the water for quenching his thirst and washing his dirty linen. The smaller the island, the more obvious it would be that access to all natural resources must be the inherent right of every person.

Therefore, the first major stipulation in the island constitution, as it should be in any socio-economic contract, should be a **prohibition against any person or any group building fences around any natural resources and so precluding their availability to all others.** Such stipulation should carry the corollary provision that all natural resources are an inheritance that belongs equally to oncoming generations and those living are simply custodians and users during their own particular lifetime.

Broadly speaking, there is only one other major economic stipulation that should be set down by the islanders protecting each citizen in his inherent rights. It would be this: **No person or group shall exercise a power that dictates or limits the amount of effort that either an individual islander or the entire island community can expend toward his or its economic and cultural betterment.** There is nothing complex about this stipulation. It is simply setting down that every person shall have the same opportunity to partner up with nature. For wealth, in every describable form of goods and services, is always some combination of raw stock and refining of that raw stock.

As our first economic stipulation carried a corollary, so should this second stipulation. It should be that all the contributions in perfecting tools and advancing science should be an inheritance of each succeeding generation, thus protecting the accumulative process of knowledge up the centuries. Like raw stock, accumulated know-how becomes an inherent right of every new-born child.

In a most fundamental sense, the foregoing cardinal points and the two basic stipulations on inherent rights provide for a workable organized society. The important consideration is that it doesn't make any difference how complex or sophisticated the society is, these premises or stipulations cannot be violated without resulting injustice. To the extent that they are adhered to, a society enjoys social justice, upholds "law and order," and makes progress commensurate with its ever-increasing knowledge.

When the history of this nation is viewed in retrospect, it is apparent that the people were left constitutionally unprotected from the growth of artificial entities that would buy up the nation's natural resources and productive machinery. Simultaneously, they would emasculate the people's inherent political power to shape their lives.

It is often said that people get the kind of laws, government and society they deserve. In the final analysis this is true, but it only underscores the fact that the supreme power rests with the people to make all changes in their affairs. More realistically, the people get the kind of laws, government and society that is in direct ratio to their supine acceptance of that which they don't understand. Not for a moment would people endure hardship or bureaucratic fiat if they grasped how both could be dispensed with summarily. They are unable to grasp that the extent to which their lives are restrained or enhanced is directly dependent on the wisdom the people exercise in imposing their own governmental discipline.

The paramount prerequisite of any constitution, premised on the "consent of the governed" is to set down the inherent rights of the citizens. These are inviolate to each and cannot be abrogated. It then provides for the legislating, interpreting, and execution of such laws—civil right—that shall reflect, protect and enhance all the inherent rights of each and every citizen. All such functioning is the role of government. Government is subservient to the constitution which in turn is subservient to the people.

The National Game of Life

Perhaps using the analogy of a baseball game will make our differentiation clearer and better understood. In the great national pastime are found all the basic ingredients making for organized governmental structure. We can identify the players as the people, the rule-book as the constitution, the umpire as the government, and the ball park and the playing equipment as the natural resources. If you will permit us slightly to stretch your imagination, we can make the ball game uncannily analogous to the whole scheme of equitable human relationships.

Let us set the stage by considering the outer boundaries of the entire United States as a gigantic ball park with 200,000,000 citizens engaged as of the present in playing the game of life. Having this picture in our minds, let us telescope our nation down to the regular size of a ball park and reduce the entire population to twenty ball players. By sheer coincidence, this makes each player symbolize ten million of his fellow citizens.

Is it difficult for anyone to make the first observation that the desire to play, the capability to play and the will to play are all vested, and reside, in the twenty ball players themselves? Doesn't it follow that whatever rules are adopted, or whatever supervising authority they may set up, must by sheer necessity and circumstance stem from their decision? In the terms of democratic government, we would say that the supreme power rests with the players.

For the sake of developing our analogy, let us assume that they are not in possession of any standard rule-book and must therefore formulate rules of their own. Right here enters the most basic-basic premise for all human relationships whether pertaining to ball players or the entire citizenry. It is that the rule-book, or the constitution, shall first set down the inherent rights of each player. These are the rights which each person is born with as an endowment of the Creator.

In the case of our ball players, the enumerated inherent rights seem elementary but are nonetheless of vital importance. They are simply the right of every player to equal access to the ball-park itself, and to the available equipment, and the right to perform with the same opportunity in accordance with the same rules. In short, no player can be denied his inherent right to participate.

Since we have twenty players, it is apparent that we have just the right number of players to make up two conventional teams with the two extra men participating as umpires. How many of our hypothetical ball players would agree to rules, or rulings, which gave advantage to some players and handicapped others? Can you envision the majority of players being denied access to gloves so that they would have to catch grounders and line drives barehanded? Or that they would have to take their turn at plate with half-length bats or no bats at all? What chance for equal performance would exist if the majority were compelled to circle all the bases in order to score and the few only had to run to first base and home, or didn't even have to leave the dugout in order to tally runs? And what if an umpire could be influenced to discriminate against the majority because it was in his interest to kowtow to the few who had garnered the equipment and rated highest on the scoreboard?

It should be patent to everyone that the foregoing circumstance would be susceptible to every form of resentment, hate and violence. In the parlance of baseball, if such inequitable conditions persisted, the inevitable outcome would be one whopper of a "rhubarb"! When we consider it in the framework of a society, or a nation, we are witness to economic and political breakdown, and the degrading of the dignity of man. In more specific terms, the denial of equitable participation can be translated into the millions out of work, tens of millions in poverty, millions denied education and medical care, millions forced into crime or mental breakdown unbearable pressures, and an entire society meandering, nationally and internationally, without purpose or hope.

In the case of the ball player, he can refuse to abide by unjust rules which don't reflect his natural right to participate and take leave of the ball-park society. He can seek out some other group, in some other neighborhood, and there find just and meaningful participation. A people making up a nation, or even more pointedly, a world, have no such escape. They are bound in their movements by the confines of the nation, or the globe, and within such limitation must work out all adjustments in human relationships.

Unable to participate in society with equal opportunity, the individual will withdraw into a condition of apathy, succumb to a psychology of complete despair, and become increasingly indifferent to what happens to himself or his nation. Or he will irrationally protest his lot in the form of crime.

Dynamics of Revolution

If the majority are unable to rectify existing inequities through established processes for redress of grievances, because such "legal" processes are no longer responsive to the rights and wishes of the people, then there remains but "illegal" protest against usurped and prostituted authority. Such open rebellion is justified, as it must be, on the premise that there exists no other recourse by which to restore the natural, or God-given, rights of the people.

It is in the Declaration of Independence that we find the most basic of basic thinking that should underlie all social contracts. Such thinking was the forerunner to our own Constitution. The heart of that political thinking is this:

> We hold these truths to be self-evident, that all men are created equal, that they are endowed by their Creator with certain inalienable Rights, that among these are life, Liberty and the pursuit of Happiness. That to secure these rights. Governments are instituted

among men, deriving their just powers from the consent of the governed. That whenever any Form of Government becomes destructive of these ends, it is the Right of the People to alter or abolish it, and to institute a new Government, laying its foundations on such principles and organizing its power in such form, as to them shall seem most likely to effect their Safety and Happiness.

Thomas Jefferson, third president of the United States, who is credited with the writing of the Declaration of Independence, consistently voiced his opposition to tyranny in all its forms. Millions of Americans can now visit the Jefferson Memorial in the nation's capital and read his dynamic words which encircle the inside of the Memorial:

I have sworn upon the altar of God eternal hostility against every form of tyranny over the mind of man.

In that same Memorial we find these words indelibly inscribed:

I am not an advocate for frequent changes in laws and constitution . . . But laws and institutions must go hand in hand with the progress of the human mind, as that becomes more developed, more enlightened, as new discoveries are made, new truths discovered and manners and opinions change.

With the change of circumstances, Institutions must advance also to keep pace with the times. We might as well require a man to wear still the coat which fitted him when a boy as civilized society to remain ever under the regimen of their barbarous ancestors.

Thomas Jefferson by no means stood alone in championing the supremacy of the people to make all change that effected justice and safety for all the people. Consider these words of

Abraham Lincoln, voiced in his first inaugural address, on March 4, 1861:

> This country with its institutions belongs to the people who inhabit it. Whenever they shall grow weary of the existing government, they can exercise their constitutional right of amendment, or their revolutionary right to dismember or overthrow it.

In our own times we have these words by President John F. Kennedy:

> Those who make peaceful revolution impossible will make violent revolution inevitable.

Here in a few words by some of the nation's most respected leaders we have highlighted the essence and purpose of all constitutions, and the constant revolutionary right of the sovereign people.

Revolutionary or radical thinking will always exist in society. When the current majority finally accepts radical ideas now propounded, then there will be a new radical group looking beyond. Radicalism, in its most constructive sense, is simply the forerunner of improvement in human relationships or in any field of knowledge.

What is radical today is the commonplace of tomorrow. It is increased knowledge and perspective that demand change and growth in all ideas and social arrangements.

The justification of civil disobedience can only be determined by the consideration of the "law" itself. Laws are man-made and neither the authority to make a law nor the power to execute a law in themselves make the "law" just or worthy of obedience.

How can there be respect for a "law" if that law is disrespectful of those whose conduct it would regulate? Constructive civil disobedience is refusal to obey unjust law. Such "law" actually **creates** injustice instead of **preventing** it.

To deny the right of civil disobedience is to deny citizenry the right of challenging tyranny! Open rebellion can assume either a passive or an active role against man-made laws or institutions. When such revolt embodies actual refusal to obey existing laws, the action is identified as "civil disobedience." When a revolt assumes the form of force, it is identified as "revolution." Bearing in mind that we are speaking of open rebellion against existing laws and government that deny full and impartial exercise of inherent rights, both passive and active rebellion are a direct appeal to Conscience and Nature as superseding all manmade authority.

If we have presented with clarity our thumbnail blueprint of the relative parts making for social structure, one overriding thought should be paramount in your thinking. It is this: **Constitutions and governments derive all authority from the people they serve and such delegated authority is for the sole purpose of protecting and insuring the equal rights of every individual citizen.**

Whenever government, laws, or constitutions do not reflect this purpose they automatically deny themselves all claim to mandatory obedience.

If every person fully understood the rights of every other person, and conducted himself in light of this understanding, there would be no need for either constitutions or governments. This would be a condition wherein man displayed, or discharged, his incumbent responsibilities on the same level as his rights. In the individual this would be the optimum in personal behavior. In society this would be the achievement of the applied brotherhood of man.

Supremacy of the People

It is extremely important that you have clearly understood the basic thinking just covered. If it were grasped by the majority of people, half the battle would already be won in restoring the nation to rational and just human relationships.

The bedrock premise for all human relationships is: **In the hands of the people themselves rests the constant supreme power to shape their lives and their destiny**. This inherent power, and this power alone, gives life to a constitution and the government that is established. By the very nature of its creation, no constitution, no government, no office can have a greater power than the people who created it. It is unadulterated usurpation when any of these thwart or go contrary to the wishes of the majority of the people. In short, in the hands of the majority rests the perpetual power to modify their constitution, eliminate it completely, or bring into being an entirely new constitution.

To the timid the foregoing is equated as a disregard for established law. To those who enjoy abnormal power and privilege, it would be equated as incitement to revolution. There is no validity to either reaction. The timid have become so conditioned by tradition, however unworkable, that they have lost identity with their own birthright. The privileged, on the other hand, have become so blinded by their acquisition of, and lust for, advantage that they have come to accept that the ability to overlord others carries with it the right of subjugation. One thing is certain: Neither from timidity nor from prostituted power will the "consent of the governed" triumph.

It is time for the American people to make candid and courageous appraisal of the Constitution and update it to be consistent with the technological age of potential abundance. It is time the people discarded their timidity and began to exercise the absolute sovereign power that is theirs in full recognition that the prime essence of a constitution is to protect equally the inherent rights of every human being within its jurisdiction.

Wasn't it the framers of the Constitution themselves who had something to say about "the dead shall not govern the living!"

A Free Society

At this point, we can postulate the prerequisites of a free society. **A free society would be one in which every solitary individual had the fullest exercise of all inherent rights, limited only to the same opportunity accorded to all others.** By this definition we can evaluate all laws, all institutions, all forms of government, and all human relationships of any organized society. We must simply ask:

1. To what extent is the right to life of every individual preserved and protected?
2. To what extent is every individual permitted to expend effort, or share in productive capacity, in applying all science to turning Nature's bounty into material products and services?
3. To what extent is every individual permitted to be a participant in society, pursuing knowledge, developing innate abilities, and exercising sovereignty in government?
4. To what extent is all mankind permitted to live their lives in peace, free from all forms of violence?

Conversely, it can be postulated that any society which deliberately or needlessly lessens the exercise of any of the foregoing inherent rights is not a free society. When such violation takes on serious proportions, as at present, the people have become the victims of a slave society. No amount of idealistic extollings, or comparisons with the victims of other lands, can alter the indictment that must be made.

To this point in the history of this nation the people have failed to work out basic human relationships so that the people have been the direct beneficiaries of the tools that have been perfected and the knowledge that has been expanded. Instead of mankind's enjoying an increased freedom, commensurate with its expanded tools and knowledge, just the reverse has come to pass. The strain and stresses of life, and its burdens, have actually multiplied. Social structure, both economic and political, have not been worked out so that every individual has had maximum exercise of his inherent rights.

The history of mankind has been largely the science of "things", with not enough thought given to man himself. The New Order in human relationships that is being ushered in must be a science of human beings. It should be premised not only on full exercise of all inherent human rights, by every solitary individual, but it should embrace a goal accentuating the man.

Through increased knowledge of all that surrounds him, and full utilization of what he perfects and uses, man will then recognize and accept his role as an integral part of a lush and vibrant Universe. Such awakened consciousness will seek equilibrium with Nature's laws and heartbeats. Herein lies man's natural expression of justice, compassion and brotherhood.

Human beings are not outcasts on the universal sea of life to be tossed meaninglessly about, with neither ballast nor direction. They need not swim continuously against the current. They can be Voyagers Unafraid who are in harmony with the troughs and crests of all evolving change.

This is the essence and the real quest of man.

Chapter 20

THE ABSOLUTE POLITICAL SOVEREIGNTY OF THE PEOPLE

D URING the political witch-hunts of World War II, two FBI agents knocked on the door of the home of a doughty little old lady who lived in Kansas. "We are the government!" they introduced themselves, in tones calculated to overawe. "Well," responded the doughty little old lady thoughtfully, "you are mistaken. **I am the government! You are my servants**. What did you want to see me about?"

It is not important here to relate that the FBI agents were following orders out of the Justice Department in Washington to interrogate good, law-abiding citizens whose only lawlessness was that they were reading literature not approved by the encumbent Administration. What is important is that the little old lady not only understood the subordinate relationship of government to the sovereign people but she had the intestinal fortitude to express such understanding to those engaged in usurpation.

Intestinal fortitude! This is what the people need. It is not sufficient in itself to recognize simply that they possess both the inherent and constitutional power to shape their lives and their destiny. There must be the will to exercise that power collectively. There must be the intelligence to do it constructively.

No crisis solves itself.

The Supreme Court has clearly ruled that "one man, one vote" is the underlying premise for all exercise of political citizenship. This positive declaration by the highest court in the land gives legal status to the inherent right of every citizen to be a meaningful participant in all that bears on and affects his life.

Our concern now is to consider the specific political reforms that must come about in order to establish the **absolute** and **supreme** power of the people politically.

Of course, parallel with political sovereignty must come the realization of economic sovereignty which we will commence to consider in the next chapter. Neither can exist without the full exercise of the other.

True political sovereignty of the people cannot be achieved without three major innovations:

1. Direct nomination of candidates by the people without the political screening of the power structures.

2. The power to elect must carry with it the power to recall any elected candidate who fails to carry out his contract with the people.

3. The sovereign people must assume direct decision-making on all laws and major policy.

Candidates of the People

If there is one obvious fact that has registered with the average voter, it is that no candidate has a chance of election without access to huge funds for underwriting campaigns. While millions of dollars are needed to underwrite presidential and senatorial campaigns, tens of thousands are needed to run for the less glorified office of U. S. Representative. Political mavericks, or Poor persons, have little chance of getting elected, irrespective of their honesty, dedication or competence. Candidates to be successful must come via the route of major political parties. And the political parties make sure of one thing above all else: No one gets their okay who shows any disposition to plead for fundamental adjustments in society.

It is in light of this circumstance that presentation of candidates to the electorate should be a function of society itself. The only requirement for a person desiring political office should be that he can obtain a reasonably-determined number of voters vouching for his candidacy. In short, all candidates should be nominated by petition, and direct primary should determine all final candidates.

However, it is the presentation of the candidates to the electorate as a public function, giving every candidate equal opportunity to present himself and his views that is the important innovation needed in by passing the undemocratic role of political parties.

The far-reaching potential of television makes the foregoing innovation possible and meaningful. It is now possible to bring every candidate into the living room of every citizen. In the case of those not having television sets, public places could be designated so that no one would be excluded from being informed. However, the future society being envisioned will consider a television set along with telephone and radio as much of an elementary necessity in every home as the stove upon which the family meal is prepared.

The important consideration here is that every candidate is directly nominated by the people and then in turn all contending candidates appear together in open forum, particularly on television, and all such costs are underwritten by government through its sovereign people. Political parties are obsolete and unnecessary. In the public interest they must be dispensed with.

To those who might he disconcerted by the idea of no political parties, let it quickly be added that in actuality there would be one political party and that would be the **people themselves**. In fact, this sovereign party has always existed, but has laid dormant, permitting artificial entities to usurp and misdirect its power.

When we come to appreciate the removal of the corrupting influence of power out of the whole economic structure, we will understand that simultaneously both the spoils of office and the tyranny of office will be removed from the whole political machinery of government. The umbilical cord giving life and sustenance to political parties will have been severed.

Power to Recall

The sovereign power to choose and elect candidates must at the same time include the power to recall any officeholder who breaks his contract with the people. Political history is replete with men who upon assuming office openly violate their campaign pledges. The electorate has been helpless to terminate abuse and malfeasance in office despite the officeholder's deliberate disregard of the people's wishes.

Just as a majority vote will put a person in office so should a majority vote remove that same person from office if he breaks his contract with the people. The right of recall must be an intrinsic part of any sovereign people's political structure.

Democracy in Action

Making it possible for any citizen to be a candidate for office, free from the dictates and dependency of political parties, and giving him equal opportunity to present his qualifications and platform could be immediate realizations. But this is only a feeble first step compared to what could be done in making every person a participating and decision-making citizen. It is now within our reach, employing our best technology, to make full democracy a practical reality.

Through the use of television in conjunction with the computerized telephone, all voting and decision making could be done directly from the home. In an address to the National Automation Conference, New York World's Fair, on July 16, 1964, David Sarnoff, Chairman of the Board of the Radio Corporation of America, had this to say in respect to the technical potential for full democracy:

In the future it will be technically feasible for voting to be done in the home with maximum personal convenience. The balloting would be done by television, the computerized telephone, standard and high-speed phone circuits of regional and national computers. For the dwindling minority of citizens who might still lack these units in the home, special telephone polling places would be provided.

Balloting would take place within a specified time period, at the voter's convenience. The individual would set his television receiver to a special voting channel and view a demonstration of the procedure to be followed. He would then identify himself over the telephone by transmitting his personal code number to the regional computer. This would be verified in the computer memory, along with his eligibility, before a pushbutton vote could be cast, and there would be safeguards against voting frauds.

Within minutes after dosing time, the regional computers would forward the data to national computers serving as central tabulators, and results would be announced less than an hour after the closing of the home polls. At the same time the computer would provide detailed analyses of the election for use on the airways and in the press. By these means, it could be possible to achieve an almost total expression of the popular will by those qualified to vote.

In a democratic society, other significant possibilities are inherent in such a system. For example, a computerized process similar to that used in home voting could obtain a prompt expression of public opinion on a wide range of issues. We could have national, regional or local plebiscites on anything from a proposed municipal tax to a contemplated change in the latest model car.

It is in light of the foregoing technical ability of the citizenry to constantly direct and run their own government and formulate their own policies that we want to stress the major innovation that must ultimately be embraced if the people are to be truly sovereign. It is this: **The inherent power of the people should be exercised directly and absolutely in the passage of all legislation and in the adoption of all major policy.**

This would be the culmination of a true democratic society. For the first time, the people themselves would be the arbiters of their own well-being and destiny. Government of the people, by the people, and for the people would have become a dynamic actuality and not just an "idealism" to which politicians gave lip service.

In practical operation, what would such a majority-rule government provide? Would it mean, as some fear, that the most intelligent in our midst would be excluded from affording the nation the benefit of their greater knowledge and skills? By no means. In fact, a political environment would exist within which the most intelligent could play roles free from the pressures of the unscrupulous and predatory in society.

Mark this important contrast: Whereas candidates for office are now dependent for their re-election on the political machines, and thereby must do their bidding. Under a circumstance where the people ruled supreme the candidates would be directly responsible to the people. All public offices would attract only those who were motivated to serve the betterment of society.

The real safeguard would lie, of course, in the final decision-making prerogative exercised by the people. The most intelligent and highest qualified would be elected to office for the purpose of **recommending** legislation and policy. All such proposals would be the result of extensive research and investigation, guided by the representatives' pledges to the people at the time they were candidates for office. Then, at an appropriate time all their findings would be presented to the people, along with their legislative proposals. The **final judgment**, or decision, would be made by the sovereign people.

The lessons of history have been cruel and exacting, in both treasure and blood, when people have delegated to a few the unchecked power to make all decisions. Overwhelmingly, it is borne out that the tendencies to criminality and corruption are more evident in the rulers than in those ruled. No society, considering those where a reasonable amount of education is available, can reach any heights of morality and material blessings until power has its widest dispersal.

Of course, it must be recognized that geographical and communication barriers did exist at the inception of this nation, and during the larger part of its history, that made it unfeasible for the people to exercise the full decision-making power. In this era of advanced technology in instant communication, verbally and pictorially, there is no necessity for a delegation of power. For the first time, the tools exist by which the sovereign people can retain the full power, the exclusive power, of decision-making.

Also, for the first time in the nation's history, the sovereign people can have perpetual television coverage of government in operation. During the past two decades, there has been spasmodic coverage of special joint sessions of Congress and special hearings of Senate Committees, but this is not sufficient. Not only should there be constant television coverage of Congress in session but there should be full coverage of both state and local representatives when conducting the public business.

Television coverage would not be so much surveillance as it would be communication between the sovereign people and those elected to serve. In fact, all of the innovations we have advanced would create a real *esprit de corps* between the people and their elected representatives.

Majority Rule

The greatest distortion and fiction of history has been the calculated propaganda that majority rule must be equated with mob rule. Those who have always sought to disadvantage the people have known that while the few can be corrupted, it is impossible to corrupt the majority. A fully informed people, each voting his own self-interest, will display rationality and be moved by both a sense of justice and compassion.

The first consideration in understanding the functioning of majority rule is that a social contract or constitution enumerates the non-negotiable, or inherent, rights of all those agreeing to the social contract. Therefore all the decision-making, including new amendments, deal explicitly with implementation of the inherent rights of each individual. Majority rule cannot destroy the basic rights of any minority—let alone that of any individual.

The second consideration is that the corruption that befalls societies stems from the corrupting influence of power. To reduce such corruption is to disperse power as widely as possible. This is the basic purpose in taking steps toward pure democracy in which the full, and absolute, decision-making power is vested in the people by their majority vote.

It might be correctly stated that civilization, in its totality of forms, would have degenerated to the extinction of mankind if it were not for the innate rationality and goodness of a majority, however minimal in expression at times, to maintain or restore justice in human relationships. What must be recognized is that the innate goodness in man cannot find expression when there exists the circumstance of domination by governmental, social or economic power groups.

The very nature of domination is to control. To control is to deny the majority their free expression. Therefore those in power are corrupted by the very need of their control to suppress criticism which is the cleansing instrument of a free society.

The most basic argument favoring majority rule is that the largest sampling of anything, whether in chemistry, physics or human beings, brings out the basic characteristics and intrinsic nature of that which is being sampled. If we accept the innate goodness in man; then it follows that such goodness will reflect itself more positively when the majority expresses itself.

It is indeed relevant here to take a look at nature, that is, at the building blocks of nature. The scientist can identify substances in the most minute amount of material. However, as he takes larger and larger amounts, the certainty of the identification becomes apparent. So it is with people. As one takes-larger and larger numbers, the true nature of man will reveal itself.

The more one gives thought to the soundness and justice of majority rule, the more one realizes that when an individual votes his self-interest—which is the very key to one-man, one-vote—he will not vote anything destructive to himself. On the other hand, in any circumstance in which a person can vote for others, there is always the temptation to promote one's own interests at the expense of the other's which is quite a different thing.

The only just society, the only safe society, the only society that enhances the innate goodness of man, and the only society that allows for individual growth through maximum participation is a majority-rule society.

In summary, a people who are to fulfill their role as arbiters of their own lives must eliminate political parties, institute the power of recall, assume direct decision-making on all laws and major policy, and provide for constant coverage of government in operation.

Only when such innovations are embraced can the people state with honesty and practical reality, "We are the government!"

Chapter 21

AN IDEA WHOSE TIME HAS COME!

W E PURPOSELY dealt first with "social contracts" and the major steps necessary to establish political sovereignty of the people before considering the steps necessary to establish economic sovereignty so that we might highlight the inherent, the supreme, power that rests in the hands of the people to effect every change for their improvement. There can be no true political sovereignty "of, by and for" the people until there is economic sovereignty "of, by and for" the people, but the first step was to recognize that they possess both inviolately.

A hundred and fifty years ago Daniel Webster voiced a conclusion for the future that prophetically underscores the predicament of America in the latter part of this Twentieth Century. He warned as follows:

> The freest government, if it could exist, would not long be acceptable, if the tendency of the laws were to create a rapid accumulation of property in few hands and to render the great mass of the population dependent and penniless. In such case, the popular power must break in upon the rights of property or else the influence of property must limit and control the exercise of popular power.

Now consider the following statement made by Frederick Douglass, the dynamic Negro spokesman, who in his West India Emancipation speech, August 1857, had this to say about the limits of tyranny:

Power concedes nothing without demand. It never did and it never will. Find out just what any people will quietly submit to and you have found out the exact measure of injustice and wrong which will be imposed upon them, and these will continue till they are resisted with either words or blow, or with both.

The limits of tyrants are prescribed by the endurance of those whom they oppress.

These two deep-thinking men have put into concise terms the whole dilemma that confronts the nation at the present time. It is uncanny how accurately they forecast our future in terms of trends and forces they already saw at work in the nation. Just a quick scanning of our chapter on "artificial entities" bears out that we have reached the condition where the "accumulation of property in a few hands" has rendered the "great mass of the population dependent and penniless"—leaving the "popular power" as the only force for the liberation of the people.

In the second instance, Frederick Douglass has expressed in less than one hundred words the relationship of the whole military-industrial-financial-political complex to the people in terms of tyrannical power and the oppressive use of that power. Volumes could be written. Volumes have been written. In essence, however, they say nothing beyond the fact that "the limits" of power-structured systems "are prescribed by the endurance of those whom they oppress."

Point of Choice

Viewing the history of this nation in retrospect, it is incredible that the oppressed of this land—not only the black and the red but the bulk of all Americans—wouldn't have risen up long ago and brought an end to their oppression. However, people are prone to suffer overlong before giving serious thought to removal of their afflictions. A point had to be reached where the unworkableness and savagery of the whole socio-economic system would force the people to accept major alternatives or else perish.

The nation has now reached that point of choice. For the first time there is an awakening to the stark realization that the nation is in trouble, real and serious trouble. No longer can the mothers and fathers of this nation, as well as its young men and women, dismiss what is happening to their lives and to their nation, as some momentary or temporary disruption. The threats to life itself are too ominous, too dangerous, and all evidence points only to increasing insecurity.

We have become a nation so busy trying to bail out the ship of state that we are blind to the gaping holes in its hull which are causing the vessel to flounder. Bigger and bigger bucket brigades are not sufficient if the citizen-sailors are to survive. And when complete frustration and despair overwhelm those made to fetch and carry, there should be no surprise that mutiny finally develops.

To the clear of mind, it is no shock that we as a people have reached the present crisis in the affairs of this nation. It was only a matter of time until private capitalism would result in such oligarchic control that the whole economy would become stultified. Subsidy, welfare, ever-mounting debt, bureaucracy, and confiscatory taxes would be the lot of the people. And with all such burdens would come mental breakdown, violence and the sacrifice of our finest young men in undefined wars.

More and bigger welfare programs, more and bigger lending institutions, more and bigger mental institutions, more and bigger prisons, and more and more punitive legislation are not the answer to the nation's dilemmas. All these simply treat with the victims of our society without giving any basic consideration as to why there need be any victims in the first place.

Palliatives and half-measures cannot suffice to meet the current crisis. A new structuring of society has to come into being before there can be stability, tranquility and justice for the two hundred million people making up this nation. The time is here when the "popular power must break in upon the rights of property" and make human rights paramount. Failure to do so can only lead to anarchy and the destruction of mankind through a triggered nuclear holocaust.

The point of choice is now.

Economic Goals

Before considering the actual framework that must be set up in order to establish the absolute economic sovereignty of the people, we should list the primary economic goals that we seek. The enumeration of these goals will largely be but a recapitulation of the inherent economic rights that have been covered throughout this book.

1. Every citizen, irrespective of race, creed or current status in the society, has to have a positive voice in shaping his or her economic life, and that of their children.

2. Every citizen, irrespective of race or creed, including every newborn child must have an equal claim to all natural resources, not excluding the airways and all levels of energy.

3. Every citizen, irrespective of race or creed, including every newborn child, must have an equal claim to all accumulated science and technology.

4. The insatiable drive for profits, property and power must be supplanted by mutual cooperation and the motivation to be of service to others.

5. All restraints on full utilization of the nation's productive capacity in terms of its best technology must be removed.

6. The total purchasing power of the entire citizenry—based on each person's rightful stake in the productive capacity of the nation—must be equal to the totality of goods and services available for purchase.

7. The suicidal path of militarism must be redirected to one of constructiveness both in regard to our own nation and the rest of the world.

8.   The primary economic goal must be to free every person from every form of material duress so that he may be free to exercise his creativity and to find inner satisfaction.

Sense of Direction

When one gives serious thought to the achieving of the foregoing goals and simultaneously considers the concentrated ownership of the nation's productive capacity, he recognizes that it isn't bigness as bigness that is wrong. Nor is it technology which replaces human muscles and human minds that is wrong. It simply is that such bigness and such technological efficiency are not now being employed for the maximum good life for the entire people in the nation.

What, then, must be done to bring sanity and economic justice back to the nation? As if a light had suddenly been turned on, or as if a compass had been dropped into the hands of one lost in the wilderness, a sense of direction presents itself with full impact. And what is the import of that sense of direction? It is this:

If the corporate structure has worked so successfully as a business framework for the few, what is to prevent the adoption of that same framework for operating a successful national business for the good life for the entire 200,000,000 people in this nation?

In short, why not incorporate the entire economy into a corporate commonwealth in which every human being is both a common stockholder and a preferred stockholder? Thus, every citizen would be a dividend-receiving stockholder giving him perpetual and inviolate purchasing claim against the full productive capability of the nation. As such participant, every person would have a stake **within** the nation but more importantly he would have a stake **in** the nation. The "maximization of profit"—or more appropriately the maximization of effort—would redound to all the people.

What a stroke of fate if the very business structure by which a minority has been able to gain invalid ownership and control of the nation's major resources and producing machinery is at the same time the same structure by which a whole citizenry could regain all of which they had been deprived! How doubly fortunate when economic justice and economic democracy could both be achieved within the same national corporate framework.

Certainly, if it is acceptable for powerful industrial and financial monopolies to use the principle of **incorporation** to concentrate most of the nation's wealth and assets in the hands of the predatory few, then the sovereign people as a whole have an even greater right to use the same principle for equitably and justly making the good life available for each and every citizen.

Instead of the few being capitalists, every human being would be a capitalist. Instead of private capitalism, we would have public capitalism. Instead of a national corporate **conglomerate**, a condition we are fast approaching, we would have a national corporate **commonwealth.**

A national corporate commonwealth! It is indeed "an idea whose time has come!"

Forerunners to the "Idea"

Before dealing with the justice, the humaneness, the integrity and the workability of a Corporate Commonwealth, specifically considering the reasoning and the steps leading to its adoption, we would be remiss if we didn't give credit to three Americans who advanced the "idea" years ago. In so doing, we are not unmindful that there are others who have propounded similar thinking.

We first want to salute Edward Bellamy who before the turn of the Twentieth Century wrote the book, "Equality," in which he thoroughly analyzed the unworkability of private capitalism along with advocating the nationalization of the entire productive capacity of the nation. Those who grasp the injustice and cruelty of the capitalistic economy today should be doubly impressed to read the monumental work of Bellamy who in 1897 left little unsaid in pointing out the built-in flaws of our whole socio-economic-political system.

However, Bellamy must be given credit for more than the writing of books, the most popular being "Looking Backward," and promoting for an ultimate society based on economic equality. He was a crusader in his own right and spearheaded relentless political effort toward translating his constructive thinking into accepted social reform.

He was an intellectual giant a century ahead of his time.

Only a reading of the suppressed book, "Equality," can do justice to Edward Bellamy's futuristic thinking. However we do want to include at least one short quote in this writing. Speaking to revolutionary economic change, we read on page 333 these stirring words:

> "Face about!" was the new word of command. "Fight forward, not backward! March with the course of economic revolution, not against it. The competitive system can never be restored, neither is it worthy of restoration, having been at best an immoral, wasteful, brutal scramble for existence. New issues demand new answers. It is in vain to pit the moribund system of competition against the young giant of private monopoly; it must rather be opposed by the greater giant of public monopoly. The consolidation of business in private interests must be met with greater consolidation in the public interest, the trust and the syndicate with the city, state and nation, capitalism with nationalism. The capitalists have destroyed the competitive system. Do not try to restore it, but rather thank them for the work, if not the motive, and set about, not to rebuild the

old village of hovels, but to rear on the cleared place the temple humanity so long has waited for."

Edward Bellamy never lived to see that "temple" erected, but he must go down in history as having laid one of its cornerstones.

The second man we want to salute is Congressman Charles A. Lindbergh, father of the "Lone Eagle," who represented the state of Minnesota in the U.S. Congress from 1908 to 1918. There have been many outstanding men who have throughout history challenged the despotic power of private banking but no one deserves more acclaim for his efforts than this courageous fighter. While he was unsuccessful in his battle to prevent the private banks from setting up a central banking system of 1918, he recognized and exposed the interlocking directorship that was forming between the controllers of "money" and the controllers of the nation's producing assets.

Like Bellamy, Congressman Lindbergh saw that progressively the people had been deprived of the fruits of their labor and systematically private capitalism had lodged the natural and producing wealth of the nation into the hands of fewer and fewer financial trusts. It was not surprising that both men foresaw that a day of reckoning must come when private capitalism or private trusts must make way for a public "trust" that included all the people.

Lindbergh's book, "Banking and currency and the Money Trust," has also been suppressed and kept out of circulation. We want to include just a short quote on page 144, to bear out the future outlook of this great thinker a half century ago:

Most men are in a condition of poverty now. Also, we absolutely know that the trust, as a result of the centralizing of the control of the industrial agencies and material resources, operated in connection with their juggling of credits and money have made us dependent upon the trust for employment. This is the industrial slavery that the capitalistic interests prefer to chattel slavery. If we were chattel slaves they would have to care for us in sickness and old age, whereas now they are not concerned with us except for the time during we work for them.

Knowing these facts, will the people continue to remain in such a state of bondage? Certainly not! The trusts have taught us the principle of combination. If it is good and profitable for the trusts it is good and profitable for the people. It would be better to have one great trust created by all of the people for their common benefit than to have our actions controlled by several trusts operated for the individual benefit of a few persons.

The third American who must be saluted in further advancing the concept of a nationally incorporated economy is William Dudley Pelley. In the early 1930s with the nation heading into the most severe depression this country has ever known, this nationally known writer and crusader presented for the nation's consideration a book called "No More Hunger." Between its covers was spelled out the fundamental features of a **Christian Commonwealth** in which every citizen in the nation would be a common and preferred stockholder in a national corporate economy. In a basic sense, Pelley had drawn together and updated the dual thinking of Bellamy and Lindbergh.

Tens of thousands read "No More Hunger" and saw the reasonableness and soundness of Pelley's proposals for removing the blight of hunger from the land, giving every person equity in the whole, and establishing productive capacity of the nation and establishing the absolute sovereignty of the people in shaping their lives. Perhaps his greatest contribution to economic thinking was his offering of a method by which debt-money and a circulating medium of exchange could be dispensed with, thus breaking for all time the strangling and stultifying influence of private banking.

It is understandable that "No More Hunger" like the other two books already mentioned was given the silent treatment. The forces that controlled the media of publicity did not want the people to grasp what they could do in order to effect their economic liberation. However, it has been thirty years of "cold" and "hot" wars that side-tracked any real opportunity for the people to give further considerations to Pelley's proposals. In fact, it was war itself that set the stage for railroading Pelley to prison and thus silencing his voice. He became the nation's outstanding political prisoner of the current century.

It is in light of the current explosive technology and the present trend of industrial-financial corporate conglomerates taking over the entire economy that the projected thinking of Bellemy, Lindbergh and Pelley becomes so timely. Their three books should be read in their entirety.

These dynamic men were the real forerunners of "an idea whose time has come!"

Chapter 22

ONLY THE PEOPLE CAN BE NATIONAL CUSTODIANS

MANY PEOPLE in hearing for the first time about incorporating the entire economy will allow that it sounds quite feasible. Quickly, however, they will question how it can be brought into being. Persons so reacting are of course, unaware of the present and projected concentration of the nation's entire producing assets in a handful of giant conglomerates, and ultimately perhaps only one. It is no longer a question of whether it would be possible to incorporate the entire economy. It is now only a question of **who owns** the national corporation and **who benefits** from it.

From the beginning this nation should have had public capitalism instead of private capitalism. This would have meant that the people automatically would have been stockholders, both dividend-receiving and voting, in all corporations commensurate with their inherent claims upon all natural resources and their individually earned claims as contributors and consumers. Belatedly, this is what must come to pass.

There is no difficulty in establishing that the people, even the most destitute, have a rightful ownership in the nation's technological machinery. To begin with, every child born, whether in a New York penthouse or in the most rat-infested tenement, has an inherent equity in all accumulated knowledge. It is all the contributions of the hands and brains of billions of people that up the centuries has made possible our technological ability to produce everything to abundance. The contributions of the Newtons, the Watts, the Bells, the Faradays, the Edisons, the Fermis, and all other scientists and inventors of history—all the scientific advancements in communications, in transportation, in medicine and in every other field related to productive technology—are a legacy of all the people.

The same reasoning must be applied in respect to natural resources. The Creator did not departmentalize this earth, or our nation, designating who should have access to the abundance of raw stock and the unlimited levels of energy. In the absence of any celestial division, every new-born child again irrespective of parental wealth or poverty, has an inherent right to the bounty of nature. No individual or any group has a right to build fences around the real wealth of the nation and then say to the deprived millions born in this generation, "You have simply been born at a time when the land and the assets of the nation are not up for grabs. Perhaps you can sign up for local welfare."

But it isn't just denial of the people's inherent equity in the nation's natural resources and accumulated knowledge that presents the full picture. As we have emphasized, and re-emphasized, capitalism has been a system under which the bulk of the people as consumers, taxpayers, borrowers and workers have directly or indirectly underwritten the expansion of all monopolies and given them the control of scientific know-how. Sophistication of technology has served to accelerate the process.

In light of all the foregoing, a Corporate Commonwealth becomes imperative. Not only would such incorporation of the nation's productive plant provide the total citizenry with a total purchasing power that would buy all the goods and services which our best technology can produce, which we will deal with in another chapter when we consider the functioning of the Commonwealth, but of equal importance, it would set the Corporate Commonwealth up as National Custodian of the nation's natural resources and accumulated science and technology for all oncoming generations.

National Custodian! When a person gets the full impact of a Corporate Commonwealth as a protector or reservoir for all resources and technology, he realizes that to solve our current problems is but half of the achievement. The equally great achievement is to set up an immortal economic vehicle that keeps intact, and keeps available the nation's accumulated ability to produce for every boy and girl who is born into life. Only at death does a citizen relinquish his lifetime equity.

One of the great errors of the past has been that private corporations never had conditions placed upon them limiting their immortality. As artificial entities, they have been able to transact business with all the rights of a human being, and in addition, they have had the tremendous advantage of immortal status allowing them to acquire and hold unlimited assets indefinitely.

The status of immortality can only be the prerogative and province of a national corporation such as the Corporate Commonwealth.

Just a Glimpse Into Our Natural Resources

During the months of April and May of 1967, the Subcommittee on Antitrust and Monopoly of the Committee on the Judiciary of the U.S. Senate conducted hearings and later released their report entitled, "Competitive Aspects of Oil Shale Development." Here is the opening statement of Chairman Philip A. Hart of Michigan to the members of his sub-committee:

> It is estimated that in the Rocky Mountain area, chiefly in Colorado, are oil shale formations containing an estimated 2 trillion barrels of oil—five times the world's known reserves—worth at going market price, close to 5 trillion dollars. Methods of extracting this oil are now close to practicality. Because approximately 80 percent of this oil shale is on Government-owned land, it is essential that the Government evolve policies

which will provide for the development of this reserve in a way that will best square with our commitment to a competitive economy. Monopolization of such an important national resource must be guarded against and at the same time orderly development of the reserve is essential. How the public interest can best be served and competition encouraged is a question which needs public exploration. As a result, public hearings are planned in this area.

$5,000,000,000,000 (five trillion dollars!) is the estimated value of the untapped oil shale resources that belong to the people of this nation. If we allocate this amount as an inherent share to all the people, it would mean that every person, including the most ill-clad and undernourished child in the city slums, is the rightful owner of $25,000 worth of oil shale resources. Is there any family in this nation who would be classed as destitute if it as a family of four had tangible assets worth $100,000?

Currently, of course, the major oil companies who already own 20 percent of the oil shale land are maneuvering to bring the entire oil shale bonanza under their jurisdiction, and possible ownership, thus depriving the American people of the full benefit of this tremendous natural wealth. Their efforts are to obtain leases, contracts or outright purchases. As in all other monopolies, the oil companies are maneuvering to get the taxpayers of the nation to underwrite all process research with the patent rights going to the private companies. And, of course, the subsequent profits and power that accompany monopoly. To those who don't appreciate the tactics of the oil monopolies we should refer to the findings of Professor M.A. Adelman, quoted in the report of the hearings, (p.39) as estimating that the total cost of the monopolistic practices in the oil industry to the American people is in the neighborhood of $4000,000,000 (four **billion** dollars) per year. He listed such practices as import restriction policy, restriction of supply, raising of prices, and expenses and depletion allowances in its tax structure.

However, the question that presents itself, which should be the vital concern of every American, is reflected in the following succinct statement by former Secretary of the interior Udall on January 27, 1967 when he made his announcement of an oil shale development policy:

> The public lands in the region representing the largest untapped source of hydrocarbon energy known to the world belong to all of the people and must be used for the benefit of all the people.

"Belong to all of the people and must be used for the benefit of all the people." We repeat this part of the Secretary's statement because it emphasizes a fundamental element that must be present and fully expressed in any just and equitable economy. It is that the natural resources, all the natural resources of a nation, are the inherent property of all the people. This means that not only the oil, and the oil shale but all the land, the forests, the waterways, the minerals and all the levels of energy to be found in nature, are the heritage of every newborn child along with all those now living.

It is these natural resources, coupled with our knowledge and science that add up to wealth. When we speak of providing for the food, the clothing, the shelter, the schools, the hospitals, transportation, communication and every conceivable product or service that enters into the economic life of the nation, we are dealing with this simple equation:

Natural resources plus know-how equals wealth.

The Real Wealth of the Nation

Perhaps the finest mind on the subject of real wealth is R. Buckminster fuller, research professor, southern Illinois

University. Under his supervision, six volumes entitled "Inventory of World Resources, Human Trends and Needs" have been compiled and published. At last a meticulous survey is available as to the work potential existing to do all the things that should be done to make not only this nation but the planet a good and safe place to live. On March 4, 1969, Mr. Fuller, popularly known for his invention of the geodesic dome, testified before the Senate Subcommittee on Intergovernmental Relations which was considering S. Res. 78 "to establish a Select Senate committee on Technology and the Human Environment." The following is an extract from this testimony:

I find man utterly unaware of what his wealth is or what his fundamental capability is. He says time and again, "We can't afford it." For instance, we are saying now that we can't afford to do anything about pollution but after the costs of not doing something about pollution have multiplied manifold beyond what it would cost us to correct it now, we will spend manifold what it would cost us now to correct it. That is a geometrical compounding of inevitable expenditures. For this reason I find that in satisfying humanity's vital needs, highest social priority must be assigned to the development of world-around common knowledge of what wealth is. We have no difficulty discovering troubles but we fail to demonstrate intelligent search for the means of coping with the troubles. This is primarily due to our misconditioned reflex which says that "we can't" afford to do the intelligent things. We discover with scientific integrity that wealth is simply the measurable degree to which we have rearranged the physical constituents of the scenery so that they are able to support more lives, for more days at such-and-such standards of health and nourishment while specifically decreasing restraints on human thought and action, while also multiplying the per capita means of communication and travel all accomplished without increased privation of any human. Wealth has nothing to do with yesterday, but only with forward days. How many forward days, for how many lives are we now technically organized to cope? The numerical answer is the present state of our true wealth.

I find that our wealth consists exclusively of two fundamental phenomena: the physical and the metaphysical. The physical in turn consists of two subdivisions. One is the physical-energy associative as matter and the other is energy dissociative as radiation. After science discover that when energy was lost from one system it was gained by another local system. It is never lost from the universe. Energy is inherently conserved, so the energy component of wealth cannot be depleted.

The other prime constituent of wealth, the metaphysical, is contributed by human intellect. Man's muscle has only a self-starter, button-pushing function. Man's mind comprehends and masters the energy of Niagara Falls. His muscle cannot compete with Niagara. Humanity's unique function is that of his mind's ability to discover generalized principles in rearranging the physical constituents of the scenery to ever greater metabolic regeneration advantage and metaphysical freedom of humanity. We discover that every time man makes an experiment, he always learns more. He cannot learn less. We have learned therefore that the intellectual or metaphysical half of wealth can only increase. Which is to say—net—that wealth can only increase with each reemployment; and the more intelligently and frequently it is reinvested the more rapidly it increases. This is not disclosed in any books on economics. It is not recognized by the body politic.

Buckminster Fuller—philosopher, scientist, inventor, world traveler, writer—has written too extensively for just a short quote to do any justice to his comprehensive thinking. The foregoing extract from the Senate testimony is given only to highlight the important consideration that the work potential to do things in this nation, or, more aptly, in the world is an ever-increasing ability. The natural resources, or "energy component of wealth" can be changed but not depleted. On the other hand, the know-how, or "intellectual or metaphysical" half of wealth can only increase. And, finally, wealth increases with its re-employment, increasing more rapidly as it is more wisely and more frequently invested.

The importance of understanding this work potential is to appreciate that mankind cannot truly benefit from the natural bounty that exists, in conjunction with the intellect with which man is endowed, unless it functions within a framework of human relationships that do not impose man-made restraints on human progress. This is the compelling reason that both the physical-energy make-up of the universe and the accumulating know-how must be equally and impartially available for the benefit of every human being. This realization is only possible within the structure of a corporate commonwealth.

In an earlier chapter we covered very sketchily the improvement of technology through the industrial revolutions that have taken place up to the current era of automation-cybernation. We referred to the Congressional investigation on the "Impact of Automation" which brought out the fact that if our best technology were employed, that was in 1961, only 10 percent of the entire labor force would be needed to produce both what the nation used and what it exported to other countries. In other words, a work potential then existed which if fully employed would have meant that each worker would have had to work only a four-hour week or with full utilization of the work force, and the automated equipment, ten times the amount of products and services could have been made available for the well-being of the nation.

Neither, of course, happened. The private capitalistic system does not allow for the full utilization of a nation's work potential. This is why, when we are overawed by the progress, technologically, that the nation has made in refrigeration, communications, transportation, electrical appliances of all kinds, and in productive techniques, we should realize that far, far greater strides could have been made if full technical know-how could have been employed. In terms of the millions of children who have been warped in body and mind, or died, who could have been properly fed; in terms of the boys and girls that could have been educated; in terms of the decent homes, safe cars, adequate hospitals that could have been constructed, and in terms on unpolluted water and air—all that could have resulted if our full technology had been employed—there are not harsh enough words to indict the private capitalist system.

It should also be a sobering thought for the apologists for private capitalism to reflect that the major break-throughs in technology came about only because wars have unleashed our productive energies. Even those who point to the achievement of sending men to the moon, and technologically it was a great achievement, are unmindful of the fact that private capitalism can gear itself to any task—if the people can be persuaded to pay exorbitant taxes—as long as that task doesn't mean economic independence for large segments of the society. For, without large segments of lowers, private capitalism cannot exist.

What we are trying to stress is that in this age of automation-cybernation we have entered, of almost unlimited application of machines to do work—skilled machines operating skilled machines—with man having tapped into the very core of the energy makeup of the universe, the real wealth of the nation is our **knowledge in doing things.** Our real wealth exceeds many, many times the actual cars, the houses, the factories, the refrigerators, the computers, the tractors, the skyscrapers, the schools, the hospitals, the atomic plants—the sum total of all tangible things that have already been constructed. The capability to **duplicate** many times all such tangible things is the real wealth of the people.

In the comprehensive work by Buckminster Fuller referred to above it is calculated that in 1960 every human being in North America had 185 energy slaves (the work capability of one man working an 8-hour day) available to work for him. Considering that such energy-slaves reflect technology, the work-energy available is much greater than in terms of human beings since machine capability performs work under conditions intolerable to humans. Only within the framework of a Corporate Commonwealth can these tireless "slaves" be put to work to remove all material duress from the lives of all the people.

Neither nuclear energy nor machines need be a curse to, or dehumanize, man. They can be the bridge to a totally free society.

Chapter 23

A NATIONAL CORPORATE COMMONWEALTH

T HE QUICKEST way of grasping the practical mechanics, or framework, of a Corporate Commonwealth is to take the largest manufacturing corporation in the United States, General Motors, and expand its operation to encompass the entire business of the nation. Bearing in mind that General Motors has an annual business turnover exceeding that of the State of New York, including New York City, and bearing in mind that we are in an accelerated process of inevitably leading up to one giant conglomerate made up of unrelated industries, it should not be difficult to envision a incorporation of all production of all production and services, including the services of government.

Now here is the thought to be encompassed: Just as General Motors allocates its gross total production, of let's say 10 billion dollars, for labor, management, executives, overhead, plant schooling, pension plans, research and plant expansion—so would the sovereign citizens' corporation allocate its Gross National Product of 1 trillion dollars (doubled many times with release of full technological potential) to the same general activities, including 200,000,000 citizens instead of a few hundred thousand workers and executives. Can't you see that the whole nation becomes one coordinated enterprise, meeting all costs and expenses out of its own productive potential?

Of course, there is one major difference between General Motors and a National Corporate Commonwealth. Private corporations have to go to the private banks in order to have their working capital. A Corporate Commonwealth would monetize its total production and there would be no need for bonding itself to outside entities. It would be exit for all forms of indebtedness, the scourge of interest and the whole spectrum of taxation.

A quote from "No More Hunger," on page 71, should make the foregoing premise clearer in our thinking:

> The hardest thing in the world to do, in expounding a work of this kind, is to wean men away from their subconscious reflexes and get their currents of thought flowing in entirely different channels.
>
> This inability to escape out of the old reflexes and channels of thinking, expressed by the lamentation, "Where would we get the money?" establishes that such persons have missed the whole crux and essence of this new system of Common wealth incorporation from the beginning. Let me insert a chapter here and say quite positively—
>
> The nation isn't going to "get the money" from anywhere!
>
> To begin with, there is no money as we think of it now in any way involved.
>
> We use the term "dollars," yes, but that is merely to express qualities of values. Money, instead of being currency or specie, becomes a standard of financial measurement, or evaluation, of both goods and services.
>
> The dividends in the Christian Commonwealth are not paid in money. They are paid in purchasing power that for want of a better standard of description of quantities is expressed in dollars. That purchasing power requisitions good that the whole Commonwealth has produced as a mammoth corporation, according to the compensation which the individual has earned by performing his integral part in the production of such goods. This requisitioning of goods is the ordinary process of going into a store and buying whatever is

desired, precisely as at present, and paying for the same by writing a check.

We speak of a "quart of milk." We mean by a "quart" a specified standardized quantity. No one ever saw a "quart" standing off by itself on a table as an abstract thing. There must always be a quart of something.

So in the metamorphosis of society that we are proposing for the happiness and security of our 72 million children, the time will come when men will say: "There is no such thing as a 'dollar' by itself in the abstract. You must always have a dollar's worth of something."

Today we think of a dollar as a coin of either silver or gold, Or a strip of beautifully lithographed green paper of exceptional wearing qualities. Really, however, even at the present time, these are only tokens for a dollar—little plaque of silver or gold, or a strip of tough silk-paper, as the case may be.

Similarly, when we speak of "dividends" as accruing from our stockholdings in the new Commonwealth, we are thinking in the old reflexes of dividends being profits from operations in finance or commerce that are paid to us from a surplus, the wages of business itself in the corporate form. Actually, when we speak of "dividends" in the Commonwealth, we mean those allotments of purchasing power that represent our personal compensation for what we have performed or contributed to the total social wealth.

To express it bluntly, the "dividends," both from Common and Preferred Stock paid to 108 million adults and 72 million children will not be money-sums procured from somewhere and parceled out to each individual according to his holdings. **They will be the actual sum-total of the produced goods of the whole nation, applied for, and paid for, and used, by the**

same persons who in their several capacities have produced them.

Re-read that final sentence. It is the key to an entirely new approach in striking a balance between production and consumption of all that the nation can produce and enjoy.

An "Accounting System" of Banking

With the total citizenry, and here is included not only workers in industry, but farmers, service people, executives, government employees, everybody having equity in the nation's total ability to produce everything to abundance, it should be obvious that it would at all times have earned claims, or purchasing power, against all goods and services in direct balance. More goods and more services would automatically mean a direct proportionate increase in purchasing power. Such purchasing power would be the nation's money supply.

The pertinent question then becomes: What form shall it take?

The answer lies in the complete elimination of private banking with its fallacious circulating cash and credit and the substitution of a nationwide Commonwealth Accounting System in which each citizen commands a credit-account equal to his purchasing claims against all purchasable products and services. We say, "purchasable products and services," because later we shall see that public services will fill a larger and larger role in an abundant society. The purchaser presents his own inviolate credit card as he makes each purchase, and a notation of the sale is forwarded to a Regional Accounting Bank to be deducted from the citizen's over-all credit. It is as simple as that.

The workability of this innovation has, of course, been made possible by the modern computer and electronic communication. Already the nation has taken major steps toward an accounting system of banking and we hear such system identified as a "cashless and checkless" society. At present it is wrongly engineered, wrongly controlled and based on the wrong premises. Yet in method it presages the only sound way of exercising purchasing power in a technological, abundant society.

Under a Corporate Commonwealth "money" will simply be a measurement of that claim. For a nation to contend that it can't do all the things that could and should be done because it has run out of "dollars" is just as ridiculous, just as absurd, as for the farmer to say that he can't plant or harvest because he has run out of "bushels," or for the carpenter to plead that he can't build because he has run out of "board feet," or that a nation can't construct highways because there is a shortage of "miles."

The ability of a nation to build can only be limited by its resources, tools and know-how. Measurements are unlimited. If you grasped the functioning of private banking in an earlier chapter, you should realize that private control of the nation's money supply has in reality been the power of the private banks to create simply the measurement "dollars." They have said to the government and to the people, "We will give you so many credit-dollars to measure the tangible ingredients—work and resources—that you possess so that you can combine them in providing the goods and the services that are usable." How strange that it didn't occur to the government and the people to recognize that the private bankers didn't give them one iota of resources or one horsepower in machines?

The "dollars" provided by the private hanks simply measured the assets and work capability that the government and the people already possessed. And for such service the nation and its people have placed themselves in irretrievable debt.

An accounting system of banking under a Corporate Commonwealth would remove all the cancerous growths of loans, interest, mortgages, and every other form of indebtedness that has afflicted and burdened the nation so long and devastatingly.

Department of Economic Coordination

In its simplest terms, a Corporate Commonwealth would be an economic framework within which the sovereign people themselves direct and coordinate all the nation's resources—raw stock, tools and technological know-how so that all the people can enjoy the good life commensurate with utilization of our full productive potential. It is nothing more nor nothing less.

There will be no attempt here to spell out meticulously the mechanics of how the people exercise economic sovereignty because in this explosive age of technology, many conventional concepts of worker-wage relationships will be impractical in a society producing everything to abundance by machines. However, it is important that we have a broad picture of the democratic processes by which the people would exercise absolute sovereignty over their economic lives.

The hub of the whole economic operation in the nation would be a Department of Economic Coordination. Would this be an appointed agency or bureau such as we have under private capitalism? By no means. This department (DEC) would be made up of the elected representatives of economic endeavor, either in goods or services, that operates in the nation. The number of representatives from each area of endeavor would be determined strictly on a ratio of "one man, one vote" as we have already advanced for the nation politically.

How does this Department of Economic coordination function?

It functions fundamentally the same way that a renovated Congress will function, with the DEC at all times being responsive to the wishes and direction of all the employees—both skilled and unskilled—and the consumers of the Commonwealth. While its principal operation is the coordinating of the nation's work capability to meet the over-all consuming needs of the entire citizenry, it would be departmentalized for specific duties.

Perhaps the most important sub-department would be the Agency of Work Capability. Here would be the constantly up-dated record of the Commonwealth's total resources, its actually productive plants, its total service facilities, and its present and projected research and technology. At all times the AWC would have at its fingertips the total producing capacity of the nation, not only as to workers in every field but as to actual location of facilities, the need for relocation of such facilities or the need for additional facilities. No longer would profit or control be determinants in working out the most efficient arrangement for either the producing or distributing aspects of the economy.

Closely allied with the Agency of Work Capability would be the Agency of Scientific Development. It would be the province of this agency to promote unrestricted research in every area of improving the nation's technology so as to remove every grueling and monotonous aspect of work from society, and at the same time to create more and more of Fuller's "energy slaves" both to free man and to assist him in fulfilling his more satisfying and constructive creative and cultural inner urges. Under the jurisdiction of the ASD would be not only the advancements pertaining to production and economic services. It would equally deal with all technology dealing with education, medicine, space exploration, ecology and all other fields concerned with advancing science. The finest minds in the nation would be attracted to this agency.

A third agency, the remaining major sub-department of the over-all Department of Economic Coordination, would be the Agency of Consumer Enlightenment (ACE). This agency would supplant the current wasteful, insulting, seductive role of commercial advertising. Constantly the ACE would publish or present via TV the latest scientific developments along with the suggested styles and designs coming out of research pertaining to all products and services. Just as constantly the consumers would be feeding back their likes and dislikes. Keeping the people informed, recording their responses and wishes, and making periodical surveys as to the actual material needs of the entire citizenry would be the basic scope of the Agency of Consumer Enlightenment.

It is in light of the computer—both as storer of information and as data processor—in conjunction with all the systems of communication—telephone and television—that the efficient and easy functioning of the foregoing Commonwealth agencies is possible.

The foregoing is an over-simplified presentation of how people could exercise absolute economic sovereignty. There is no attempt to pre-determine the wishes of the people as to the amount or the kind of production or services. Nor is there any attempt to pre-determine the individual desires for certain occupations, use of their leisure time, or to make any judgment as to relative worth of one group against another. The only aim and goal of a Corporate Commonwealth is to actualize an economic-social framework within which the people, all the people, can exercise positive voices in these areas.

Our broad concern is to show that the economy of the nation can be operated democratically, that all of the evils of built-in obsolescence, seductive advertising, and profit and power can be eliminated, and that everything can be produced at cost with emphasis on quality, and that all the employments of technology would give careful attention to long-range effects on our ecology and the living condition of future generations.

Strange as it may seem, the moment the idea is propounded that the people, all the people, should have their equitable share in the producing assets of the nation, in the minds of many arises the upsetting thought that an entirely new set of technical men, managers and supervisors, would replace current personnel. Nothing is more absurd. Under a Corporate Commonwealth, they would be needed more than ever. Their roles would be enhanced because for the first time their efforts would all be geared to producing quality—not built in obsolescence—and for the first time, production would be geared to meeting the needs of the majority and not to realizing power and profit for the few.

The whole idea of a Corporate Commonwealth is to liberate not only out best technically trained manpower, including our best scientist, but also our full technological machinery to create the best America of which we are capable. There is nothing inherently wrong with a highly developed technology, or with the men and women who run it. It is only a question of whether all are employed for the good of all human beings or whether they are directed in such a way as to deprive people and sabotage the whole economy.

Extent of Public Services

Economically, it must now be appreciated that if our full technology were employed, the disparity between the highest standard of living and the lowest standard of living would continually decrease. We have entered a technological age in which machines are not only replacing the mental jobs but are replacing semi-skilled and skilled occupation. In short, it is the technology, which belongs to everyone, which could account for ninety percent of our productive ability. In light of this fact, it is realistic and equitable to project a new economic order in which there will eventually be at least ninety percent economic equality amongst all the citizens.

Obviously, the first large public or cooperative service would be meeting every citizen's claim to adequate food, clothing and shelter in order to live with at least a minimum of dignity. Every child, every man and every woman would exercise this genuine claim because of his or her part ownership in the entire economy. Many forms of a guaranteed income are being promoted but none of them premise the right to them on the fact that the people have an inherent and an earned equity in the nation's capacity to produce.

Women in particular should welcome such economic independence. No longer need a truly incompatible marriage be tragically endured because of economic pressure. Neither, on the other hand, would homes be broken because of income problems nor would children wander aimlessly without supervision because both parents must work in order to meet family expenses.

Public services would be much more encompassing. Next to the food that sustains life, survival is dependent on a lifetime of medical care when sick or injured. Out of an abundant society would come a sufficiency of hospitals, clinics and nursing homes, adequately staffed and adequately equipped one of the top priorities of a compassionate society. The medical field, more than any other, would demonstrate such compassion in equal service to each and every human being.

The other major public service would be education. Each and every boy and girl must be given unlimited opportunity to expand his or her learning to the maximum extent of his or her desire and capacity. Therefore, each individual, without cost of any kind, would be afforded the opportunity to partake of all levels of education as a constant right during his entire life. The strength of any nation can be measured by the degree of its intelligence constructively applied to all aspects of society. Unstinted encouragement must be given to the growing youngster who is tomorrow's citizen, or indeed to the person of any age who desires to learn.

What must be grasped is that none of the public services of basic necessities, medical care and education are underwritten by paternalistic government. Every citizen, as a stockholder in the Corporate Commonwealth, is actually underwriting his own public services. Instead of first taxing the people, as under private capitalism with all the costs of bureaucratic-administration, the Commonwealth simply allocates from its total productive capability the material and personnel necessary to take care of the foregoing basic requirements of the citizenry.

In addition to the three major public services we have mentioned, there could be all-free transportation. There could be all-free communication. There could eventually be free services in such areas as plumbing and electrical service. When full technology would come into play—and an abundant society had been realized—the whole psychology of everyone for himself would change into one of mutual concern and the desire to help others.

Private Property

In terms of one's home and one's personal possessions, private property would be more inviolate to the individual than they are now when one's home is continually threatened by foreclosure or nonpayment of taxes. A home could not be taken from a family. All payments would be toward ownership, all forms of rent, mortgages, and interest having been eradicated out of the economic structure. More to the point, there would be no economic restraints on building millions of apartments and homes.

To those who fear that a Corporate Commonwealth would leave no room for the person who derives pleasure and enjoyment in operating a small farm, or small shop, or an individual research enterprise, it must be emphasized that there would be greater opportunity to do so. We are simply stressing that the main supply of goods and services can be supplied cooperatively, making full use of the best machines, so that maximum time would result for the individual to do exactly what he wanted to without economic compulsion. Today small operators are being forced out of business by the monopolies at a record rate.

In being a shareholder in the whole economic capacity of the nation, an individual's right to private property would take on a significant meaning. Instead of being a **momentary** owner of an individual operation **within** the society as at present, he would under a Corporate Commonwealth, be an inviolate owner of his proportionate share in the whole national operation which would last his **entire** lifetime.

Is This Socialism or Communism?

It would be neither. In socialistic and communistic countries, at least in theory, all industries are nationalized and autocratic government directs the economy. While there are many different forms of socialistic patterns, it would be fair to state that in the main it is the State which directs production by governmental policy and thereby controls the economic well-being of the people. Under private capitalism, a minority has gained control of the productive assets and in turn dictates governmental policies.

Under the Corporate Commonwealth, and this is extremely important, the ownership is vested in every solitary citizen. In other words, we are talking about **people's** ownership. We are talking about the absolute right of the people themselves to democratically shape their economic lives as well as to democratically shape their political lives.

A Corporate Commonwealth is based on making the individual paramount. It is the fulfillment of his needs, the development of his innate talents, and the achievement of his fullest freedom that takes precedence over everything else.

Actualizing a Corporate Commonwealth

The first consideration that must be entertained is that it is sheer folly to believe that any major economic and social change can be achieved by appealing to the current political-economic power structures. No abnormal power groups will sanction their own unseating.

There is only one realistic approach toward the adoption of a Corporate Commonwealth and that is the enlightenment of the people themselves. Out of such enlightenment will come automatically the political strength to order social change. Whether the political strength would display itself in pressure on existing representatives or in electing a majority of new committed representatives of the people is immaterial. In either case, an enlightened people is the first step.

To those who feel that this approach is slow and the obstacles are formidable, they should realize that there are many attendant results that are commensurate with the educational effort. Foremost is the circumstance that the very people who will be the participants in the New Order need the most encompassing understanding so that they can sustain change when it is finally achieved.

Within the framework of the Constitution itself are sufficient powers to retrieve from the largest monopolies what they have unjustly taken from the people. All that is required is a nation-wide aroused electorate to compel the Congress to act. If the elected representatives defiantly refuse to respond to the demands of the sovereign people then tyranny has replaced any semblance of constitutional government.

First, there is the **taxing power** of government. This power, implemented with price-control and the closing of tax loopholes, could force the multibillion-dollar oligarchies to return to the entire citizenry the hundreds of billions of dollars in assets that were underwritten by the nation's taxpayers, workers and consumers. The poetic justice would lie in the fact that the whole area of "administered prices" engaged in by 90 percent of all industry has been nothing but a usurped power to tax exercised by the monopolies.

Secondly, there is the whole area of **judicial determinations**, both on the part of government and by the sovereign people themselves. Already such monopolies as the largest electrical and steel companies have been found guilty of defrauding the people. Certainly there are legal approaches to bring the monopolies into court, or before quasijudicial commissions, so that a full determination can be made as to the restitution that must be made to the people.

Thirdly, there is the power of **eminent domain**. This power, alone, exercised by the sovereign people could usher in a Corporate Commonwealth. There is no need to incorporate the economy. It has already been achieved by a mere handful of industrial-financial conglomerates. All that is necessary is to make a judicial appraisal and turn it over to its rightful owners, the whole people. What would stop the sovereign people from creating their own credit-based on the future productive potential of the whole nation—and buy outright the nation's entire productive plant?

It should be emphasized that there must be fair remuneration to all individuals who have valid stock: ownership, especially in all cases where it reflects savings and earnings.

The people are absolutely supreme. They need not endure unjust and prolonged suffering. They need only to be enlightened as to the cause of their suffering. Out of such enlightenment will come the wisdom and courage to affect their liberation, and secure for all oncoming generations the right to enjoy a safe, just and prosperous society.

Chapter 24

RESPONDABILITY

T HE REAL stumbling-block to confronting and solving the problems of this nation is that there are three major realities that must be encompassed in our thinking. There is the kind of America that most people **think** we live in, there is the kind of America that we **do** live in, and there is the kind of America that we **could** live in. Not until a majority encompasses all of these realities will there be sufficient understanding by which to effect social change that is just, sound and lasting.

Reduced to its simplest dimensions, we have tried to convey the inescapable picture that the major problems that beset and burden the nation are man-made problems. We have tried to present, as a corollary, that a sovereign people don't have to endure these problems one moment longer than the day that they understand the remedial measures to be adopted.

People don't have to live in poverty, men don't have to be without work, homes and farms and businesses don't have to be foreclosed on, children don't have to be drop-outs from school, and a whole people don't have to pay tribute to a financial despotism that has put a whole nation in bondage.

Above all, boys and young fathers don't have to be sacrificed in needless wars in order to build "military-industrial-political" complexes into permanent war machines.

These are all aspects of the servitude that has befallen the nation.

What should shock us down to the marrow of our bones is the realization that we have become a nation of 200,000,000 Americans who have become insensitive to the dangerous threats to all life that is posed by our environment. Overlong delay in solving our problems and providing for meaningful roles for every human being has already led to an irreverence for life itself. We have lost the ability to respond to protecting not only our wellbeing but our very safety and survival.

We are not talking about responsibility. This is secondary. We are talking about something that is even more basic. We are talking about **respondability**. This is the ability to respond with sensitivity to the injustice and the suffering in the society. It is the ability to translate statistics into human beings. It is the ability to place oneself in the plight of others so that their agonies become one's own.

But it isn't just the ability to respond to iniquities and hardships. This is only half the reaction that must be evinced. Even more importantly we need the respondability to what must be done to solve all problems. And in so responding we must be able to recognize that it has been the "system" that has been at fault. All behavior and conduct, however arrogant or despotic, have simply conformed to the compulsions of that system.

The important outlook is that everything is not lost. There is real hope for the future if we will recognize that every human being is important, that we live in a Good Universe, and that we, the people, constantly have the power to effect constructive change.

Across the breadth and length of this land of ours are tens of millions of our fellow citizens who have lost all faith in the future, either for themselves or their children. They must be aroused out of their apathy to the poignant realization that they can have a new lease on life. A New Order amongst all men awaits only their endorsement.

Those currently involved in violence, crime and rebellion must grasp that they are wasting their energies in futile and costly protest. Constructively channeled, such force could give real impetus to achieving a meaningful and prosperous and safe life for every human being in America.

Respondability! This is the dynamism of life itself. It needs only to be rekindled and guided purposefully!

BIBLIOGRAPHY

University Press, New York, 1959

Government

—*The Declaration of Independence*
—*The Constitution of the United States*
LOCKE, JOHN *Treaties on Government*
ROUSSEAU, JEAN JACQUES *The Social Contract*
PAINE, THOMAS *The Rights of Man*
BEARD, CHARLES A. *An Economic Interpretation of the Constitution of the United States,* Macmillan, 1961
BRANT, IRVING *The Bill Of Rights, Bobbs, Merrill.* Indianapolis, 1965
DOUGLAS, WILLIAM O. *The Anatomy of Liberty,* Trident Press, New York, 1963
MILLS, C. WRIGHT *The Sociological Imagination,* Oxford
PADOVER, SAUL K. (editor) *Thomas Jefferson on Democracy,* D. Appleton-Century, New York, 1939
RUSSELL, BERTRAND *Political Ideals,* Simon & Schuster, 1964
SOROKIN, PITIRIM and WALTER LUNDEN *Power and Morality,* Porter Sargent, Boston, 1959
Spooner, Lysander *No Treason,* Pine Tree Press, Larkspur, Colorado, 1966
UZZELL, THOMAS H. *The Twilight of Self-Government,* Bruce Humphries, Boston, 1961

Economics

BAGDIKIAN, BEN H. *In the Midst of Plenty,* Beacon Press, Boston, 1964

BAZELON, DAVID T. *The Paper Economy,* Random House New York, 1959

BELLAMY, EDWARD *Equality,* D. Appleton, New York, 1987

DOUGLAS, C.H. *Social Credit,* Eyre & Spottiswoode, London, 1937

HARRINGTON, MICHAEL *The Other America, Macmillan,* New York, 1962

MAY, EDGAR *The Wasted Americans, Harper & Row,* New York, 1964

PELLEY, WILLIAM DUBLEY *No more Hunger,* Aquila Press, Noblesville, Indiana, 1961

THEOBALD, ROBERT *The Rich and the Poor,* Clarkson N. Potter, New York, 1960

THEOBALD, ROBERT *The Challenge of Abundance,* Clarkson N. Potter, New York, 1963

THEOBALD, ROBERT (editor) *The Guaranteed Income,* Doublesday, New York, 1966

WEBER, MAX *The Protestant Ethic and the Spirit of Capitalism,* Translated by Talcott Parsons, Charles Scribner's Sons, New York, 1958

Corporations and Their Control

BEARD, CHARLES A. *Jefferson, Corporations and the Constitution,* National Home Library Foundation, Washington D.C. 1936

FULLER, JOHN G. *The Gentlemen Conspirators,* Grove Press, New York, 1962

GALBRAITH, JOHN KENNETH *The New Industrial State,* Houghton, Mifflin, Boston, 1967

GOODMAN, WALTER *All Honorable Men,* Little, Brown, Boston, 1963

GOULDEN, JOSEPH C. *Monopoly,* G.P. Putnam's Sons New York, 1968

HACKER, ANDREW (editor) *The Corporation Take-over,* Harper & Row, New York, 1966

Kefauver, Estes *In a Few Hands: Monopoly Power in America,* Random House, New York, 1965

Lundberg, Ferdinand *The Rich and the Super-Rich,* Lyle Stuart, New York, 1968

Lundberg, Ferdinand *America's Sixty Families,* Vanguard Press, 1938

Means, Gardiner *The Corporate Revolution in America,* Crowell-Collier, 1962

Mills, C. Wright *The Power Elite,* Oxford University Press, New York, 1959

Myers, Gustavus *History of the Great American Fortunes,* Modern Library, New York, 1907

Ridgeway, James *The Closed Corporation,* Random House, New York, 1968

Stern, Philip M. *The Great Treasury Raid,* Random House, New York, 1962

Ziegler, Edward *The Vested Interests,* Macmillan, New York, 1964

Money and Private Banking

Adams, Silas Walter *The Legalized Crime of Banking,* Meador Publishing Co., Boston, 1958

Baumgardner, Raymond C. *Our World Without Money,* Guadalajara, Jal., Mexico 1967

Congregational Union of Scotland MONEY—A *Christian View,* Glasgow, 1962

Dwinell, Olive Cushing *The Story of Our Money* Meador, Boston, 1946

Federal Reserve Board *The Federal Reserve System: Purposes and Functions,* Published periodically by the Federal Reserve Board, Washington, D.C.

Hattersley, C. Marshall *Wealth, Want and War,* The Social Credit Co-ordinating Centre, Yorks., 1937

Lindbergh, Cong. Charles A. *Banking, Currency and the Money Trust, 1913* Edition, reprinted by Omni Publications, Hawthorne, California, 1968

Morton, Frederic *The Rothschilds: A Family Portrait,* Curtis, (Antheneum), New York, 1962

Overholser, Willis A. *The History of Money in the United States,* Progress Publ. Concern, Libertyville, Ill., 1936

Soddy Frederick *Wealth, Virtual Wealth and Debt, Omni Publications,* Hawthorne, Cal., 3rd Ed., 1961

Vickers, Vincent C. *Economic Tribulation,* Omni Publications, Hawthorne, California, 1960

Voorhis, Jerry *Out of Debt, Out of Danger,* Devin-Adair, New York, 1943

Technology

De Latil, Pierre, *Thinking by Machine,* Houghton, Mifflin, Boston, 1957

Ellul, Jacques *The Technological Society,* translated by John Wilkinson, Alfred A Knopf, Inc., New York, 1964

Fuller, Buckminster *Ideas and Integrities,* Prentice Hall, Inc., Englewood Cliffs, N.J., 1963

Hilton, Alice Mary (editor) *The Evolving Society,* The Institute for Cybercultural Research, New York, 1966

Michael, Donald N. *Cybernation: The Silent Conquest,* Fund for the Republic, Santa Barbara, Calif., 1962

Wiener, Norbert *The Human Use of Human Beings: Cybernetics and Society, Doubleday,* New York, 1956

Military and Foreign Policy

Beard, Charles A. *The Devil Theory of War,* Vanguard Press, New York, 1936

Beard, Charles A. *President Roosevelt and the Coming of the War, 1941,* Yale University Press, New Haven, 1948

Cook, Fred J. *The Warfare State,* Macmillan, New York, 1962

Davis, Jerome *Peace, War and You,* Henry Schuman, New York, 1952

Davis, Jerome and Hugh B. Hester *On the Brink,* Lyle Stuart, New York, 1959

Fall, Bernard B. *Last Reflections on a War,* Doubleday & Co., New York, 1964

Fulbright, J. William *The Arrogance of Power,* Vintage Books, Random House, New York, 1966

Lapp, Ralph E. *Kill and Overkill,* Basic Books, Inc., New York, 1962

Lapp, Ralph E. *The Weapons Culture,* W.W. Norton & Co., New York, 1968

Mills, C. Wright *The Causes of World War Three,* Simon and Schuster, New York, 1958

Mollenhoff, Clark R. *The Pentagon,* G.P. Putnam's Sons, New York, 1967

Pauling, Linus *No More War,* Dodd, Mead & Co., New York, 1958

Report from Iron Mountain Dial Press, New York, 1967

Wise, David and Thomas B. Ross *The Invisible Government,* Random House, New York, 1964

Race Relations

The Autobiography of Malcolm X Grove Press, Inc., New York, 1966

Carmicheal, Stokeley & Charles V. Hamilton *Black Power,* Random House, New York, 1967

Cleaver, Eldridge *Soul on Ice,* McGraw-Hill Book Co., New York, 1968

King, Martin Luther, Jr. *Where Do We Go From Here: Chaos or Community?* Beacon Press, Boston, 1967

Stampp, Kenneth M. *The Peculiar Institution,* Random House, New York, 1956

The Report of the National Advisory Commission on Civil Disorders (The Kerner Report) E.P. Dutton & Co, New York, 1968

General

Berton, Pierre *The Comfortable Pew,* J.B. Lippincott, Philadelphia, 1965

Ford, Henry *My Life and Work,* Doubleday, Page, New York 1922

Pike, James A. *If This be Heresy,* Harper & Row, New York, 1967

Shapley, Harlow *Of Stars and Men, Beacon Press,* Boston, 1958

Wright, Frank Lloyd *Writings and Buildings* (Selected by Edgar Kaufman and Ben Raeburn) Meridian Books, World Publishing Co., Cleveland, 1960

Senate and House Reports and Hearings
United States Government

Hearings before the Select Committee on Nutrition and Human Needs of the Unites States Senate, Ninetieth Congress, Second Session (1968-1969)

Hearings before the Sub-Committee on Antitrust and Monopoly, Committee on the Judiciary, United States Senate, Eighty-Eighth Congress, On Economic Concentration
Part I Over-all and Conglomerate Aspects (1964)
Part II Mergers and other factors affecting industry concentration (1965)

Hearings before Sub-Committee of the Select Committee on Small Business, United States Senate, Ninetieth Congress, Second Session on Planning, Regulations, and Competitions Automobile Industry (1968)

Hearings before the Sub-Committee on Economy in Government of the Joint Economic Committee, Congress of the United States, Ninetieth Congress, Second Session on Economics of Military Procurement (1969)

Report of the Sub-Committee on Economy in Government of the Joint Economic Committee, Congress of the United States, Ninetieth Congress, Second Session, The Economics of Military Procurement (1969)

Hearings on the IMPACT OF AUTOMATION ON EMPLOYMENT *before the Sub-Committee on Unemployment and the Impact of Automation, of the Committee on Education and Labor, House of Representatives, Eight-Seventh Congress, First Session,* (1961)

Hearings on COMPETITIVE ASPECTS OF OIL SHALE DEVELOPMENT *before the Sub-Committee on Antitrust and Monopoly of the Committee on the Judiciary, United States Senate, Ninetieth Congress, First Session* (1967)

Hearings before the Sub-Committee on Intergovernmental Relations of the Committee on Government Operation, United States Senate, Ninety-first Congress, First Session, on S. Res. 78 To ESTABLISH A SELECT SENATE COMMITTEE ON TECHNOLOGY AND THE HUMAN ENVIRONMENT (1969)

Hearings before the Sub-Committee on Domestic Finance, of the Committee on Banking and Currency, House of Representatives, Eighty-Eighth Congress, Second Session on the FEDERAL RESERVE SYSTEM AFTER FIFTY YEARS, 3 VOLS. (1963)

A PRIMER ON MONEY (1964)